The UAB
Marcel Proust Symposium

The UAB
Marcel Proust Symposium

In Celebration of the 75th Anniversary of *Swann's Way* (1913-1988)

Edited by

William C. Carter

SUMMA PUBLICATIONS, INC.
Birmingham, Alabama
1989

Copyright 1989
University of Alabama at Birmingham

ISBN 0-917786-75-0
Library of Congress Catalog Number 89-62847

Printed in the United States of America

Frontispiece photo of Marcel Proust courtesy of Roger-Viollet, Paris

Contents

Foreword

During fall term 1988 at the University of Alabama at Birmingham (UAB), the School of Humanities sponsored a major celebration of Marcel Proust, his work, life, and times. The occasion was the 75th anniversary of the publication of *Du côté de chez Swann (Swann's Way)*, the first volume of *A la recherche du temps perdu (Remembance of Things Past)*, considered by many writers and scholars to be the greatest novel of the twentieth century. The essays printed in this volume are those presented at UAB by distinguished writers and scholars, many of whom are among the world's most renowned in Proustian studies.

During the Marcel Proust at UAB program, which lasted from September through November, exhibitions and events related to Proust were held at UAB and in other educational and cultural institutions, such as the Birmingham Public Library and the Birmingham Museum of Art.

The largest art exhibition, *Fin-de-siècle Faces: Portraiture in the Age of Proust,* was on view in the UAB Visual Arts Gallery. This exhibition brought together paintings, drawings, photographs, costumes, furniture, and Proust memorabilia from major French and American museums and from private collections here and in France. The portraits of Proust's parents, Dr. and Mrs. Adrien Proust, were loaned to the exhibition by the Proust Museum in Illiers-Combray, France. The UAB show marked the first time these portraits were exhibited in America. Odile Gévaudan, daughter of Proust's famous housekeeper, Céleste Albaret, loaned many items from her mother's collection, most of which had never before been exhibited. The catalogue for the exhibition was written by its curator, Professor Heather McPherson of UAB's Department of Art. The show opened with a slide lecture by Katell le Bourhis of the Costume Institute of the Metropolitan Museum of Art; Ms. le Bourhis's topic was "Proustian

Scenes, Social Codes and Dress: A Key to the Belle Epoque." Special guests at the opening were Mr. Didier Destremau, French Consul General, New Orleans; Mr. Philippe Albou, attaché culturel, New Orleans; Professor Philip Kolb, Honorary President of the American Proust Society; Ms. Anne Borrel, Secretary-General of the Société des Amis de Marcel Proust, France; and Odile Gévaudan.

The Birmingham Museum of Art created an exhibition of thirty photographs by Jacques-Henri Lartigue: *Fashion and Adventure: The France of Jacques-Henri Lartigue and Marcel Proust*. The photographs dating from Proust's period were selected because many of Lartigue's subjects were those about which Proust wrote. Each photograph was accompanied by an appropriate quote from *Remembrance of Things Past*. This exhibition was curated by Sherrie Gauley.

UAB's Sterne Library, holder of one of the world's largest collections of Proust material, including a recent acquisition of fifteen letters, offered two exhibitions: a *Proustiana Exhibition,* featuring the letters from the UAB Proust Collection, as well as Proust letters, telegrams, photographs, personal effects, and documents loaned by Odile Gévaudan, and other Proust manuscripts and letters on loan from the University of Illinois Library. The second exhibition housed in Sterne Library, *Marcel Proust: A Landscape Portrait,* consisted of fifty-four photographs of Proustian places by noted French photographer, François-Xavier Bouchart. These photographs, each of which is accompanied by quotes from Proust selected by Elyane Dezon-Jones, were the subject of his book, *La Figure des Pays*. Mr. Bouchart was a special guest during the Proust term and the trip to Birmingham was his first visit to the United States. This exhibition has since traveled to galleries in Memphis and New Orleans.

Taken together these exhibitions made up the largest collection of Proust material ever exhibited outside of France.

In addition to the exhibitions, other events in Marcel Proust at UAB included dance programs, a benefit piano recital of music from Proust's epoch, a reading of passages on music from Proust, a concert reading by members of the Birmingham Festival Theatre under the direction of Frank Trechsel, and a showing of all the major films inspired by Proust and his work. A special course on Proust was taught by William C. Carter and J. Theodore Johnson, Jr., of the University of Kansas, who was Visiting Jemison Professor during the Proust term.

We were extremely pleased to have members of the Proust family as our guests during the Proust celebration. Mr. and Mrs. Patrice Mante-Proust and their daughter, Patricia, made their first trip to the United States to Birmingham to visit the Proust exhibitions and to attend the concert reading at the Birmingham Festival Theatre. One of our speakers, Nathalie Mauriac Dyer, who is the great niece of Proust, gave her first public lecture on the writer at UAB.

Marcel Proust at UAB received extensive local, regional, and national publicity, including a report on National Public Radio. It was also selected to be an official event in the American Celebration of the Bicentennial of the French Revolution.

Major sponsors of Marcel Proust at UAB were the Birmingham Festival of Arts Salute to France 1988-89, the Alabama Humanities Foundation, Friends of UAB Department of Art, Friends of Sterne Library, and the Alliance Française of Birmingham.

These essays are printed in the order in which they were presented at UAB. Two of the contributors, Professors Elyane Dezon-Jones and Jean Milly, preferred to submit their written essays in French.

Anne Borrel, in her essay, "Céleste and the Genius," traces the relationship of Céleste Albaret and Proust. Céleste became Proust's housekeeper in 1914 and remained in his service until the writer's death in November 1922. The writer was devoted, as is evident from his letters and the tributes paid to her in *Remembrance of Things Past,* to Céleste and members of her family, who were in a way adopted by Proust. The relationship that developed between these two very different people contained a great deal of humor, complicity, and kindness. Professor Borrel quotes the texts from *Remembrance of Things Past* where portraits of Céleste and members of her family are given, including a portrait of Proust himself as seen by Céleste. This portrait constitutes one of the most obvious intrusions of the author into the narration of the novel. Ms. Borrel spent many hours with Odile Gévaudan, daughter of Céleste Albaret, listening to the taped interviews that were the basis of Céleste Albaret's award-winning memoirs, *Monsieur Proust.* Ms. Borrel's article gives us new information about Céleste and her family and contains some previously unpublished material. The telegrams that Proust sent to Odilon Albaret and his correspondence with the Larivière family were on view in the *Proustiana*

Exhibition at UAB. Ms. Borrel's lecture was followed by a showing of Percy Adlon's film, *Céleste*, with Odile Gévaudan as a special guest.

Roger Shattuck presented his talk, "Trouble and Transparency in Marcel Proust," in the form of a clever dialogue among a philosophy professor who is also the author of a book on Proust, a recording studio operator, a graduate student in French, and a free-lance radio journalist. The group sets out to determine the five laws of thought as they are found not only in Proust's novel but in the creative imagination. All the discussion leads up to the question, "If we can't communicate, why write? why read?" In supplying an answer, Professor Shattuck refutes Paul de Man's interpretation of a famous passage from Proust about the narrator reading in a garden. The text published here is, among other things, a penetrating essay on the experience of reading, one of Shattuck's and Proust's favorite topics and obviously central to a true understanding of how literature works and what happens when we read—and why we have such affection for books. This essay has a surprise ending.

Elyane Dezon-Jones, in "La Réception d'*A la recherche du temps perdu* aux Etats-Unis," gives a brief but valuable history of the publication and reception of Proust's novel in the United States—a subject appropriate to the tribute being paid to Proust and his work by an American university. She corrects oft-repeated errors about the history of Proust's novel in America and reveals the little-known fact that the first translation of a Proust text in English appeared not in Britain but in an American literary magazine in 1920. Professor Dezon-Jones is thorough in her reporting on the Proustian landscape in America, covering not only the history of the first translations of Proust in English and Proust's influence on major American writers but also early contributions to Proustian studies by American scholars.

Nathalie Mauriac Dyer recently published with Etienne Wolff a previously unknown typescript of *Albertine disparue* with manuscript corrections that are among the last made by the novelist. The typescript was discovered in the papers of her grandmother and Proust's niece, Suzy Mante-Proust. Ms. Dyer's essay, "The Death of Albertine," explains how this typescript dramatically affects the concluding sections of *Remembrance of Things Past* in its present form. If Proust had maintained the cuts and revisions indicated on the typescript, he would have had to alter radically subsequent sections of the novel. This discovery establishes beyond a doubt that Proust's final choice for the title of this section was *Albertine* *disparue* and not *La Fugitive*. The newly discovered version of *Albertine disparue* is a key Proust document as Ms. Dyer maintains and sheds new light on the unifying elements of the plot, illuminating the hidden structure of the novel.

Richard Ratzan, M.D., is a practicing physician who has developed an interesting side speciality in the humanities and medicine. In his essay, "*De Motu Cordis* and *Swann's Way*: Exploring the Circulatory System of Proust's Narrative Technique," Dr. Ratzan combines medicine and literature as he compares Proust's narrative technique and naturally occurring structures in the physical universe. The body of the novel becomes a living corpus as Dr. Ratzan examines space, time, and the function of the human circulatory system in light of the style and structure of Proust's organic text. Ratzan's comparisons reveal fascinating parallels between the structure of Proust's novel, Proustian sentences, and the circulatory system of the human body. He also proposes additional investigations into the microstructure of the text. At the end, Dr. Ratzan demonstrates how the narrator has become the pacemaker cell of *Remembrance of Things Past*.

J. Theodore Johnson, Jr., who contributed a paper on "Proust's Referential Strategies and the Interrelations of the Liberal and Visual Arts," sees Proust as a bold and didactic artist who was influenced by Greek and medieval philosophy and architecture through the mediation of works by John Ruskin and Emile Mâle. In those texts, art is seen as pleasure and instruction. Professor Johnson brings to bear in his article topics on which he has lectured and written extensively: visual arts, architecture, and the novel as cathedral. Examining the encyclopedic, universal nature of *Remembrance of Things Past*, Professor Johnson proposes a method of reading Proust inspired by the novelist's own ideas on etymology. The essayist invites the reader to look deeply into this text that is so full of rich allusions.

Jean Milly, who was prevented by illness from attending the UAB Marcel Proust Symposium, sent a written essay. In 1987, just prior to the Proust celebration at UAB, new editions of *Remembrance of Things Past* appeared in France. Jean Milly is the general editor of the ten-volume edition of *A la recherche du temps perdu* for Garnier-Flammarion, one of the most accessible and useful editions of Proust to date. Richard Howard has chosen Professor Milly's edition for the text upon which he will base his new American translation of Proust, a translation that will restore Proust's own title: *In Search of Lost Time*. Here Professor Milly gives a brief

history of the publication of Proust's volumes, the specifics of the manuscripts published to date, statistics of the extensive sales of *Remembrance of
Things Past* in France, and information about new translations. He also
discusses some of the problems posed by the edition of *Albertine disparue*
published by Nathalie Mauriac Dyer and Etienne Wolff.

Philip Kolb traces for us the history of comparisons between
"Shakespeare and Proust," beginning with the title of the current English
translation of Proust's book, *Remembrance of Things Past*. Proust,
according to readers' surveys cited by Professor Kolb, now occupies in
France the same exalted position as Shakespeare in English literature.
Professor Kolb examines those elements that make a truly great writer, and
particularly the basis of Shakespeare's reputation, in order to see if a comparison between Shakespeare and Proust has merit. In his informative
examination of Proust's qualities as a writer, Professor Kolb compares the
two writers' use of vocabulary, characters, structure, style, metaphors,
poetic expression, and psychological insights.

Wallace Fowlie gave the closing lecture of the UAB Marcel
Proust Symposium on the subject that had been the basis for the entire celebration: the seventy-fifth anniversary of the publication of *Swann's Way,
1913-1988*. His lecture, "Swann Is Seventy-five Years Old" takes as its
text the line in *Remembrance of Things Past* indicating that the major events
in the hero's life can be traced back to his acquaintance with Swann: "The
subject matter of my experience, the subject matter of my book, came to me
from Swann." Professor Fowlie examines Charles Swann in his human
relationships, particularly with the narrator, and connects these to the meaning of the entire Proustian universe. Professor Fowlie believes that Swann
is Proust's favorite character and likens his role in relation to the narrator to
Virgil and Dante in *The Divine Comedy*.

A ll of these essays are eloquent testimony to the vitality and
universality of *Remembrance of Things Past*. From the day *Swann's Way*
was published in 1913, Proust was on his way to being recognized as a
major literary figure. His winning the Goncourt Prize, France's major
literary award, in 1919 for *A l'ombre des jeunes filles en fleurs (Within A
Budding Grove)* brought fame that has endured. Although there have been
periods of apparent neglect, the sales figures, translations—thirty-eight
different languages to date, among which new translations in American,

Chinese, and Italian—five new French editions since 1987, monographs and adaptations in various media that continue to proliferate, leave no doubt that Proust is a great universal writer. Marcel Proust at UAB was an exhilarating celebration of this writer and his work.

On behalf of UAB, I would like to thank all the writers whose work is printed here not only for these essays, which form a permanent record of their contributions to our celebration and Proustian studies, but also for their appearances at UAB during the Proust term and for remaining with us to attend classes, visit the Proust exhibitions, and meet faculty, students, and people from the community. Their talents, interest, and enthusiastic support were major factors in the success of Marcel Proust at UAB.

Finally, I wish to thank the UAB School of Arts and Humanities and especially its dean, Theodore M. Benditt, for making possible the publication of this volume.

William C. Carter
Project Director, Marcel Proust at UAB
University of Alabama at Birmingham
November 1988

1

Céleste and the Genius

Anne Borrel

ON A DAY IN APRIL 1913, Odilon Albaret, a taxi driver frequently hired by Marcel Proust since 1907, takes his young wife of two weeks to 102 boulevard Haussmann. Odilon tells Mr. Proust that he is back on duty and may be called again. In the kitchen, glowing red with the roaring furnace and the copper saucepans on the walls, is a couple: Nicolas, Proust's man-servant, and Céline, Nicolas's wife, who welcome the new Mrs. Albaret to Paris. The visitor tries to make a good impression but is silent and shy, wishing to leave as soon as possible. She is too awed to see or hear anything.

A few months later, during her second visit, a man looking much younger than his forty-two years enters the kitchen. He seems tall and slim, a simple jacket over trousers and white shirt give him a look of supreme elegance; his hair is dark with a curious little curl on his forehead; he has beautiful skin and teeth; gracefully he takes Mrs. Albaret's hand, saying: "Madam, let me introduce Marcel Proust, in casual attire and beardless."

Céleste Albaret had heard the name of Marcel Proust for the first time on her wedding day, March 17, 1913. Just before she and Odilon left to go to the church, he had received a warm telegram of congratulations from one of his customers. "I knew he was quite an extraordinary man," Odilon had said, "and quite different from other people, but I would never have expected him to cable me his wishes." And now in this kitchen, Céleste sees that this young lord is the extraordinary customer, but she does not understand a word of this introduction: Mr. Proust's beautiful black beard had been shaved off the day before.[1]

Who was Céleste Albaret? Who was the Marcel Proust who meets her in 1913 and with whom she is going to live until his death in 1922? If this meeting is important for the life of the young lady, how important is it to the work of art that is at that time in the hands of the genius and beginning to be published?

All the visitors, journalists, admirers, or friends of Marcel Proust who wanted to recollect the genuine perfume of the "Temps perdu" visited Céleste between 1924 and 1958 at the Hotel d'Alsace-Lorraine near Saint-Sulpice; then, in the sixties, when Céleste took up residence in the composer Maurice Ravel's house, they made their pilgrimages to Montfort-l'Amaury in the Rambouillet Forest. After Céleste had spent so many years in the service of Marcel Proust, it is hard to imagine her running a modest hotel in Saint-Germain-des-Prés or taking care of an informal museum such as Ravel's house. From the time of Proust's death, November 18, 1922, she kept reliving her memories, which were inhabited by a genius who first appeared in her quiet life "in casual attire and beardless."

At that time, 1913, Céleste was twenty-two. Born at Auxillac, Lozère, on May 17, 1891, she grew up in this village in the center of France, amid the brooks and steep slopes of forests. Her parents owned a water-mill with a seven-acre farm that for centuries had been the estate of her father's family, the Ginestes. A hugh vellum parchment preserved in the archives of Mende (the main town of Lozère) dated 1620 shows the map of the property with the name of the owners. In the farmhouse, under which ran a stream, the familial atmosphere was hearty and warm. Let us imagine, for instance, one day in the year 1896. Ten people are sitting around the table in the main room (the Gineste family is a big and generous one): between the parents and grandparents is the eldest son Régis, born belatedly in 1879, nine years after his parents' wedding. Then at three-year intervals there followed two sons, Paul and Joseph, then two daughters, Céleste and Marie, then the last son, Julien, born in 1894. The maid, the stable boy, and two farmhands also share this warm atmosphere. Céleste, at five, is already a tomboy; she climbs trees, steals bird nests, makes holes in her shoes and stockings, tears her dresses, and tyrannizes her sister, who adores her. She is very active and temperamental, changing from a shrew to a charming girl in a moment.

Céleste's childhood and youth are happy. Her parents are not poor and they cherish their children. She and her sister are educated at the nuns' boarding house in the next small town, La Canourgue. But in 1897 a series of disasters begins, the first of which is the burning of the farm mill. Her mother, pregnant at that time, delivers a last son who would not survive. Then, in 1901, another tragedy: the eldest son Régis dies. He was something of an inventor and artist, spending his time experimenting with new techniques for photography, printing, and so forth. He had become a civil servant in a Parisian suburb. After a bicycle accident, his mother went to nurse him; then, knowing nothing would help, he came back to Auxillac to die. He was twenty-four, Céleste was ten. Régis's approaching death was a matter of conversation in the family, even with him. Two years later, the last terrible event of Céleste's youth occurred: she lost her beloved youngest brother, Julien, who died at the age of nine from heart rheumatism. Céleste would always remember her mother's wish: may you never see your children die before you.

But this is the way life goes, and Céleste was never bitter; the memories she kept from her childhood were strong and cheerful. She remained close to every member of her family as long as they lived and after. Years later when she had a new house built on the site of the old farmhouse, she had occasion to return periodically to her native village.

Suddenly, at fourteen, Céleste ceases to be a tomboy. Nothing, then, would have made her go out. She stays home all the time, experimenting with sewing and embroidery, occasionally reading popular novels, and dreaming. She and her sister never go to the fields since their brothers and the servants helped the parents run the mill and farm.

Céleste had become a tall, beautiful young lady, looking over the surrounding world with dreamy eyes and a romantic pout. She would remain lost in her thoughts for hours, forgetting her needle or book. Were those thoughts dreams of love? Not really. Marriage was far from her mind. She believed that she would spend her life just as it was then, with her beloved parents, brothers, and sister, and could not imagine a different way. She thought that this happiness would be her life forever.

Céleste had known Odilon Albaret for several years, as he was a frequent visitor of her cousins, but she had never thought of marrying him. He was ten years older than she and worked as a Parisian taxi driver, a position that impressed everybody in the family. Odilon and Céleste began to write to each other. His mother had died when he was twelve years old and he had had a rather hard childhood; she loved her mother tenderly and her youth had been a happy one. Odilon found in her both comprehension and sweetness. It was Odilon's sister, Adèle Larivière, who was also living

in Paris and owned with her husband a prosperous café near the boule-
vards, who played the role of matchmaker. She spoke to the cousin and
eventually visited the Ginestes to make all the arrangements. Odilon came
from Paris just for the wedding, and it was then that Céleste heard for the
first time the name of Marcel Proust as the sender of the following telegram:
"All good wishes and congratulations, I do not write at length because I
suffer from influenza and I am tired but I pray with all my heart for the
happiness of you and yours."[2]

Odilon Albaret had planned that after the honeymoon in their new
flat in Levallois, he and his young wife could buy a business in Paris, as his
brothers had already done. He had saved enough money to set up as a café
owner, as did most of the Auvergnats in the capital. He continued to hire
his taxi to good clients, such as Proust, who called him by phone. Odilon
thought his young wife needed time to get accustomed to her new life and to
Paris; he encouraged her to visit his brother Jean and sister-in-law Adèle in
order to get used to the business, but she remained timid. Nervous,
frightened by everything, she became more and more languid.

At the end of August, Marcel Proust asked Albaret how was his
young wife. "Not very well," answered Odilon, "she has lost weight, she
does not sleep, she hardly visits her in-laws. Of course, I am not at home
very often, but she does not seem to worry about that." Proust listened,
then diagnosed: "She misses her mother," and, he added, "Why not ask
her, in order to distract her, if she would like to deliver messages for me?"
Odilon reported the conversation and suggested to Céleste that she might go;
he finally had to insist and she came to 102, boulevard Haussmann the day
after the beard was shaved off, in the beginning of September 1913.

The meeting of Céleste and the genius nearly coincides with the
publication of *Du côté de chez Swann* in November 1913. In fact her first
service to Proust was to distribute the autographed copies around town.
She would come over and receive a message or parcel from Nicolas for her
to deliver. This work was indeed a distraction for her, although she would
have denied having any grief or need for such distraction. In any case,
Céleste says from that time her life changed completely: there had been a
time "before Proust"; there would never be for her a time "after Proust."

Very soon Proust was using Céleste not only as a "runner" but also
as a telephonist[3] and maybe as an interlocutress who would be another
means of observation for him. After she had finished delivering *Swann*,
Proust started to converse with this curious woman and get to know her

better. This can be seen, for instance, in a letter to Reynaldo Hahn circa January 29, 1914, in which Proust quotes verses of a poem by Sully Prudhomme: "Ici bas tous les lilas meurent." Céleste had learned this poem at school and Proust copied three strophes for her, which she carefully preserved. Both of them liked the last stanza: "I dream of couples who last / forever. . . ."[4]

Proust's correspondence since 1914 shows the different aspects of Céleste and Proust's relationship. In everyday life, Céleste is used as a reliable messenger: she is sent for money, she brings letters, she makes all phone calls from the little café next door after Marcel gave up his line in order not to be disturbed. She is more and more necessary to Marcel, who cannot stay alone and who is unable to manage any of the details of everyday life. As the war has begun, all the men are gone. Proust suggests that Céleste could take Nicolas's bedroom as a temporary solution: "Madam, I am infinitely grateful for your condescending to take care of a sick person; it is impossible for you to stay here a long time, since it is not proper for a man who spends his miserable existence lying in bed to be looked after by a lady and particularly a young lady." And he adds: "Of course, Madam, I know perfectly well that you do not know anything and you are unable to do anything; so, I shall ask only that you prepare my coffee extract, which is the most important thing." Then, staring at her: "You don't even know how to use the third person form of address." She had no idea what he meant by this, so she answered: "No, Monsieur, and I shall never know."[5]

In the following years Proust's letters would confirm her domestic incompetence, which seemed to vary according to the mood of the improvised chambermaid or to her stage of exhaustion. Proust sometimes mentions the "errors of the zealous messenger."[6] To his friend Lucien Daudet, Proust writes, for example, in 1915: "I have read your letter, Céleste put it in its place, impossible to find it again"[7] or "she is too much 'Clara d'Ellebeuse' [the heroine of a novel] for everyday life (though I like Clara d'Ellebeuse very much)."[8] Even worse: to Paul Morand in March 1917: "I was dreadfully sorry when I became aware that Céleste let me go out with soap on my shirt and an old waistcoat. What could the wonderful lady have thought of me?"[9] (It was Proust's first meeting and dinner party with Princess Soutzo at the Ritz.)

In 1919 Proust, who does not want to let Céleste visit his old friend, Madame Catusse, complains to the latter: "Céleste is broken by excessive fatigue (. . .) which makes her insufferable towards me. . . ."[10] To another old friend of his mother's, Madame Straus, he writes in 1918: "Céleste is really a little foolish: she had three million things to ask you about and she forgot them all, and now she leaves me with a dry inkpot and I do not know where to find any ink. . . ."[11] In 1921, in a letter to his English friend Sydney Schiff, we witness a familiar drama. There has been a crossing of letters and Proust fears that the longest letter he wrote in answer has been "destroyed" since it is impossible to find it anywhere: "After all, Céleste thinks," writes Proust, "that since she had marital problems [des soucis conjugaux] that evening, she might have thrown it inadvertently in the garbage can," and he adds "our reciprocal thoughts may have been the prey of a scavenger."[12]

In spite of her peculiar temper, or because of it, Proust soon showed a deep affection for Céleste, as he confesses in the above-quoted letter to Madame Catusse: "This is not to complain about her whom I like very much. . . ."[13] Proof of his affection is given in telegrams and letters of condolence sent in 1915[14] and in his famous dedication of 1921 to the fourth volume of *La Recherche:* "To my dear Céleste, to my faithful friend of eight years, but in reality so involved in my thoughts that I should daresay my friend of always, being unable to imagine that I have not known her forever, knowing the former spoilt child through her present caprices. . . ."[15] As for Céleste, she became at once completely devoted to this man who understood her so well and in whose life she soon became entirely involved with perfect contentment.

At the outset, Proust mentions her as "Madame Albaret"; for instance in the letter to Reynaldo Hahn, August 30, 1914: "In such circumstances, I think I can perfectly well take Madame Albaret with me to Cabourg; she proposed to dress up as a man, which I refused, though she could act as a Countess Chevreau very well."[16] After the mobilisation, when Céleste had definitely, and in a way naturally, settled into Proust's apartment, he starts to mention her as "ma femme de chambre" or "Céleste." She becomes a general housekeeper as Marcel Proust writes in 1915 to Madame de Caillavet: "The charming and perfect chambermaid who has been these last few months as well a valet, a nurse,—I would not say a cook, except for herself, as I do not eat anything. . . ."[17] Céleste reports in her taped memoirs that she would occasionally be asked to prepare eggs "à la crème," or a fried Dover sole, or a compote. When Marcel felt like having a special dish or sweet, he would send Céleste to the specific restaurant or provider whose quality and service he knew to be the best. He had to obtain what he wished immediately, since he was unable to stand the shortest delay. Sometimes, after one taste, the dish would be rejected: "This is not the taste I remembered."[18]

It seems to be a matter of some amusement that Céleste is taken for Proust by the persons she calls on the telephone: "Is that you, Marcel?" Some friends are upset with the perfect resemblance of voice, but many of Proust's friends admire "La belle Céleste" very much. Lucien Daudet thought she was Swedish; thus Proust often refers to "the fake Swedish girl" or "ma femme de chambre, l'Auvergnate que vous croyiez Suédoise."[19] He seems to appreciate her distinction and beauty: "Céleste, the beautiful creature who serves me as a chambermaid"[20] or "my chambermaid, delicious person who is the niece of the Archbishop of Tours and resembles Lady de Grey forty years ago."[21] He also calls her "Jeanne d'Arc, Récamier, Botticelli."[22] He writes for her "tender and pretty verses"[23] when he discovers that her brother has married the niece of an archbishop. He writes proudly that she is "the niece of the Archbishop of Tours" but in the verses he describes her as "Grande, fine, belle, un peu maigre, / Tantôt lasse, tantôt allègre, / Charmant les princes et la pègre, / Lançant à Marcel un mot aigre. / Rendant le miel pour le vinaigre, / Spirituelle, agile, intègre, / C'est la presque nièce de Nègre" (Nègre is the name of the archbishop).[24]

This Céleste "is literally celest(ial)" as Marcel puns[25] and as time passes, a certain intimacy develops between the two, "each of us in his place" Céleste would say fifty years later. Marcel Proust quotes Céleste's observations to his correspondents and relies very much on her advice. For example, in November 1914 (speaking of an aristocrat): ". . . he has a really graceful simplicity, which even struck my chambermaid. . . . She told me 'What simplicity for a noble man!' "[26] In 1917, speaking of a man that Proust had not met himself: "Céleste liked him but she found he looked frivolous (elle lui a trouvé l'air léger). This portrait is enough for me. . . ."[27] When thanking André Gide for sending him a copy of *Les Nourritures terrestres,* Proust does not hesitate to echo the extraordinary spoken pastiche Céleste gave of the book, but he fails to mention that both of them laugh at the imitated style.[28] This humor about their special relationship can also be perceived in a letter to Jacques Rivière: "Céleste keeps my letters in boxes. She is in bed now; I am too (not in the same bedroom), so I cannot find your letter"[29] or to Paul Morand: "This looks a little like a declaration. What would Céleste say!"[30] To Princess Soutzo, in

1917, Proust shows Céleste as a true confidante and witness: "My attachment for you has become a suffering and only Céleste has been able, for some time, to perceive its acuteness" or "I spent some time discussing with Céleste whether or not I might return to bid you good night, after which it was no longer possible to do so."[31] About the illness and the death of his friend Emmanuel Bibesco: "I had guessed and predicted everything for a long time. Céleste and maybe Morand know that."[32]

This closeness created by their daily exchanges and mutual respect also extended to Céleste's family. Proust is struck by the sorrow that Céleste shows when she learns of her mother's death in 1915: "She entered my room screaming with pain."[33] He is quite able to understand her hypersensitivity (even in other circumstances) and writes to her niece, Marcelle Larivière, who is then near Auxillac, a four-page letter of recommendations for the care of Céleste's health.[34] During and after the war, Proust takes part in the mournings of the Albarets in a warm and nearly familiar way.[35] Odilon Albaret had returned from the war rather ill: "I shall take Anginargol," writes Proust to Lucien Daudet, "the effect of which will be destroyed by the angina of Céleste's husband, who is to be hospitalized here."[36] As a matter of fact, when Odilon settles into the apartment, Proust decides to cure a serious kidney ailment the veteran is suffering from. A touching note published by Claude Mauriac in the last volume of his diary, L'Oncle Marcel, shows indications for Odilon's diet followed by a compliment to Céleste: "a cup of strong cherry-stalk tea / mashed potatoes if available / you are charming today."[37] Odilon was cured thanks to Proust's prescriptions.

Other members of Céleste's family also shared the apartment at different times. In early 1922, Proust writes to Paul Morand: "I still have my typist and as Céleste's family seems destined to swarm around me, I shall probably keep her."[38] The typist mentioned is Yvonne Albaret, Céleste's niece, who typed in 1922, in addition to many letters, three copies of Cities of the Plain—The Captive. Céleste's sister, Marie Gineste, had settled once and for all at Proust's in 1916, after a short stay in 1915. So Céleste has help, but no one interferes with her service to Proust, which combines devotion, tenderness, complicity, humor, and which is, for Céleste, a station of perfect happiness.

Proust must have felt secure because of this constant and familiar feminine presence, which was benevolent, friendly, and perhaps motherlike as well as daughterly. After Agostinelli's death, on May 30, 1914, he was desperate and terribly let down after becoming aware of the cupidity and duplicity of a man he considered "being a part of (his) life."[39] He found in Céleste a reliable and comprehensive ally, intuitively conscious of the exceptional creation she was witnessing. On occasion Proust dictated passages of *La Recherche,* but she and her family also provided materials for the text. They provide names such as La Canourgue (the small town near Auxillac): Proust imagines a "Mademoiselle de la Canourgue" who is among the "good matches" for Monsieur de Châtellerault in *The Guermantes Way.*[40] Albertine's song at the beginning of *The Captive,* or the "cris de la rue," in the same part, are brought to Proust by Odilon who is asked for details. "La dissertation de Gisèle" (Gisèle's essay) [41] may have been inspired by two dissertation drafts and "résumés," which Proust thanks Céleste's niece, Marcelle Larivière, for sending. He congratulates the young lady for the perfection of her writing and syntax as well as for her knowledge.[42]

The most famous portrait of Céleste in the text is the long passage where she and her sister are drawn as "les deux courrières de Balbec" in the part translated as "Cities of the Plain." Here Proust not only depicts very accurately and penetratingly the two women with their distinct psychology and language, he also sketches scenes of their everyday life:

> ... I had very soon formed a mutual bond of friendship, as strong as it was pure, with these two young persons, Mademoiselle Marie Gineste and Madame Céleste Albaret. Born at the foot of the high mountains in the centre of France, on the banks of rivulets and torrents (the water passed actually under their old home, turning a millwheel, and the house had often been damaged by floods), they seemed to embody the features of that region. Marie Gineste was more regularly rapid and abrupt, Céleste Albaret softer and more languishing, spread out like a lake, but with terrible boiling rages in which her fury suggested the peril of spates and gales that sweep everything before them. They often came in the morning to see me when I was still in bed. I have never known people so deliberately ignorant, who had learned absolutely nothing at school, and yet whose language was so literary that, but for the almost savage naturalness of their tone, one would have thought their speech affected. With a familiarity I reproduce verbatim, notwithstanding the praises (which I set down here in praise not of myself but of the strange genius of Céleste) and the criticisms, equally unfounded,

in which her remarks seem to involve me, while I dipped crescent rolls in my milk, Céleste would say to me: "Oh! Little black devil with hair of jet, O profound wickedness! I don't know what your mother was thinking of when she made you, for you are just like a bird. Look, Marie, wouldn't you say he was preening his feathers, and turning his head right round, so light he looks, you would say he was just learning to fly. Ah! It's fortunate for you that those who bred you brought you into the world to rank and riches; what would ever have become of you, so wasteful as you are. Look at him throwing away his crescent roll because it touched the bed. There he goes, now, look, he's spilling his milk, wait till I tie a napkin round you, for you could never do it for yourself, never in my life have I seen anyone so helpless and so clumsy as you." [And Céleste ends the discussion with a word of her own: "Poor Ploumissou!" This is the word that Céleste's mother used to call her when she was a child. Then, as Céleste is arguing, she cuts the narrator short with some peculiar observations:] "Oh! The story-teller! Oh! The flatterer! Oh! The false one! The cunning rogue! Oh! Molière!" (This was the only writer's name that she knew, but she applied it to me, meaning thereby a person capable both of writing plays and of acting them.) "Céleste!" came the imperious cry from Marie, who, not knowing the name of Molière, was afraid that it might be some fresh insult.[43]

It would be necessary to quote all the passages, for example, the one about the photograph of the narrator " 'when he was little . . . dressed . . . with his little cane . . . all furs and laces, such as no prince ever wore, ' "[44] and then the photograph of himself that Proust gave to Céleste. Céleste's admiration for Proust is expressed in the text in a very realistic way, but at the same time the reader may have the impression of a disguised self-portrait of the author, as in those paintings where the painter appears himself "en abîme" in a mirror that reflects him at his easel.

"Look, Marie, he has only to put his hand on the counterpane and take his crescent, what distinction. He can do the most insignificant things, you would say that the whole nobility of France, from here to the Pyrénées, was stirring in each of his movements."

Overpowered by this portrait so far from lifelike, I remained silent; Céleste interpreted my silence as a further instance of guile: "Oh!

Brow that looks so pure, and hides so many things, nice, cool cheeks like the inside of an almond, little hands of satin all velvety, nails like claws," and so forth. "There, Marie, look at him sipping his milk with a devoutness that makes me want to say my prayers. What a serious air! They ought really to take his portrait as he is just now. He's just like a child. Is it drinking milk, like them, that has kept you their bright colour? Oh! Youth! Oh! Lovely skin. You will never grow old."[45]

And further on, " 'Look, Marie, at his delicate lines. Oh, perfect miniature, finer than the most precious you could see in a glass case, for he can move, and utters words you could listen to for days and nights.' "[46] This passage should be compared to another further on:

Alone, the curious genius of Céleste might perhaps appeal to me. In spite of myself, I would continue to smile for some moments, when, for instance, having discovered that Françoise was not in my room, she accosted me with: "Heavenly deity reclining on a bed!" "But why, Céleste," I would say, "why deity?" "Oh, if you suppose that you have anything in common with the mortals who make their pilgrimage on our vile earth, you are greatly mistaken!" "But why 'reclining' on a bed, can't you see that I am lying in bed?" "You never lie. Who ever saw anybody lie like that? You have just alighted there. With your white pyjamas, and the way you twist your neck, you look for all the world like a dove."[47]

Céleste, like Proust, had a gift for imitations: "It was, in the form of the delivery of a simple message that she had obligingly undertaken to convey, an inimitable portrait." Some anecdotes about Céleste and her sister are put in the text just as they are, without any transposition:

They never read anything, not even a newspaper. One day, however, they found lying on my bed a book. It was a volume of the admirable but obscure poems of Saint-Léger-Léger. Céleste read a few pages and said to me: "But are you quite sure that these are poetry, wouldn't they just be riddles?" Obviously, to a person who had learned in her childhood a single poem: "Down here the lilacs die," there was a gap in evolution.[48]

Even the anecdote of the uncle archbishop is in the book, with some changes because Céleste frequently referred to two different bishops: "Françoise was considerably impressed when she learned that the two brothers of these humble women had married, one the niece of the Archbishop of Tours, the other a relative of the Bishop of Rodez."[49]

One echo of conjugal tempests introduces the reader to a beautiful description of Céleste's temper and physical beauty:

> Céleste would sometimes reproach her husband with his failure to understand her, and as for me, I was astonished that he could endure her. For at certain moments, raging, furious, destroying everything, she was detestable. It is said that the salt liquid which is our blood is only an internal survival of the primitive marine element. Similarly, I believe that Céleste, not only in her bursts of fury, but also in her hours of depression preserved the rhythm of her native streams. When she was exhausted, it was after their fashion; she had literally run dry. Nothing could then have revived her. Then all of a sudden the circulation was restored in her large body, splendid and light. The water flowed in the opaline transparence of her bluish skin. She smiled at the sun and became bluer still. At such moments she was truly celestial.[50]

At fifteen, Proust wrote in Antoinette Faure's keepsake book. To the question "For what fault have you the most toleration?" he answered: "Pour la vie privée des génies" ("for the private life of geniuses"). Proust's projected essay about Sainte-Beuve, *Contre Sainte-Beuve,* had been taken up in part to combat the famous author's habit of judging writers by their social standing and mores. Céleste confirms that when Proust became aware that people could publish his letters, he feared it and tried to prevent it. In a letter of January 1921 to the Duchesse de Clermont-Tonnerre, he writes: "I absolutely desire (I shall explain to the public my reason for this in an introductory note to *Swann's Way*) that there should not be saved and published *a fortiori* a single piece of my correspondance."[51] In spite of this prohibition, we have here read and published Proust's letters. If we have used them widely it is not in order to explore "the private life of a genius," which is rather irrelevant. For a genius like Marcel Proust, the only reality is the spiritual world; when he amalgamates fragments of ordinary life, it is to transmute them by a superb alchemy into a work of art. By examining the nature of Proust and Céleste's relationship, as revealed in his letters and her memoirs, we may try to draw the basis of a further study, which would indicate, in an extensive way, which texts written or corrected by Proust between 1913 and 1922 owe something to Céleste's presence or personality. We should note that all the passages quoted above, as well as the etymology of the name "Albaret" given by Brichot in *Cities of the Plain,* are handwritten additions to a typescript of *Sodome et Gomorrhe.* The descriptive scene with the two sisters is a long addition of nine pages, the others are written in the margin.[52] In a material way, it is obvious that Céleste might have facilitated Proust's work by providing a warm and secure atmosphere and perhaps partially satisfied "this terrible need of a being" that the narrator confesses.[53] But when Proust writes, for instance, about "the living linguistical genius" of Françoise after having noted "the strange genius" or "the curious genius" or even "the personal sense of poetry" of Céleste, and when he quotes over several pages, specific expressions of Françoise's that are obviously borrowed from Céleste's way of speaking, we should seek further. A detailed examination of the different strata of the text (manuscripts, corrected typescripts, corrected proofs) may enable us to determine, as has been briefly shown here, what the text owes to Céleste. It is possible to see, in addition to a portrait of Céleste as Céleste, some traits of Céleste in other characters. We could point out such traits in Françoise, or more unexpectedly in Albertine, and even in the Duchesse de Guermantes. But that will be for another time.

Notes

[1]Céleste Albaret, *Monsieur Proust* (Paris: Editions Robert Laffont), 1973, p. 13; and Philip Kolb: *Correspondance de Marcel Proust,* tome XII (1913), 1984, pp. 267-68.

[2]Kolb, *Correspondance,* t. XII (1913), 1984, pp. 117-18.

[3]Ibid., t. XII (1913), p. 391, n. 2.

[4]Ibid., t. XIII (1914), 1985, p. 87; and *Monsieur Proust,* p. 451.

[5]*Monsieur Proust,* p. 41.

[6]Kolb, *Correspondance,* t. XIV (1915) 1986, p. 214.

[7]Ibid., t. XIV (1915), p. 226.

[8]Lucien Daudet, *Autour de soixante lettres de Marcel Proust,* Cahiers Marcel Proust, 5 (Paris: Gallimard, 1952), p. 186.

[9]Kolb, *Correspondance,* t. XVI (1917), p. 74.

[10]Marcel Proust, *Lettres à Madame C.* (Paris: J. B. Janin, 1946), p. 188.

[11]Kolb, *Correspondance,* t. XVII (1918), 1989, p. 524.

[12]*Correspondance générale de Marcel Proust,* tome III, publiée par Robert Proust et Paul Brach (Paris: Plon, 1932), p. 53.

[13]*Lettres à Madame C.,* p. 189.

[14]*Monsieur Proust,* pp. 442-44; and Kolb, *Correspondance,* t. XIV (1915), pp. 107-09.

[15]*Monsieur Proust,* cover p. 4 (reproduction); and Catalogue exposition "Marcel Proust et son temps" (1971) n° 360, f, p. 82 (à M. Pierre Berès).

[16]Kolb, *Correspondance,* t. XIII (1914), p. 297.

[17]Ibid, t. XIV (1915), p. 105, and also t. XIII (1914), p. 335.

[18]See *Monsieur Proust,* pp. 93-103.

[19]Kolb, *Correspondance,* t. XIII (1914), p. 361, and t. XIV (1915), p. 203.

[20]Ibid., t. XVI (1917), p. 282.

[21]Ibid., t. XVI (1917), p. 153.

[22]Mina Curtiss, "Céleste" in *The Cornhill,* Spring 1950, p. 308.

[23]Unpublished note, private collection.

[24]*Monsieur Proust,* p. 137.

[25]Kolb, *Correspondance,* t. XVI (1917), p. 278.

[26]Ibid., t. XIII (1914), p. 335.

[27]Ibid., t. XVI (1917), p. 146.

[28]Ibid., t. XVI (1917), p. 239.

[29]Marcel Proust et Jacques Rivière, *Correspondance 1914-1922,* présentée et annotée par Philip Kolb (Paris: Plon, 1955), p. 120.

[30]Paul Morand, *Le Visiteur du Soir* (Genève: La Palatine, 1969) p. 118.

[31]Kolb, *Correspondance,* t. XVI (1917), p. 330.

[32]Ibid., t. XVI (1917), p. 221.

[33]Ibid., t. XIV (1915), p. 105.

[34]Ibid., t. XIV (1915), p. 108.

[35]Ibid., t. XVI (1917), pp. 107-10; and *Monsieur Proust,* pp. 441-44 and p. 447 (letter of 1920 to André Larivière).

[36]Daudet, *Lettres,* p. 214.

[37]Claude Mauriac, *Le Temps immobile X — L'Oncle Marcel* (Paris: Grasset, 1987), p. 337.

[38]Morand, *Le Visiteur du soir,* letter dated 18 February 1922.

[39]*Correspondance générale de Marcel Proust,* tome VI, publiée par Robert Proust et Paul Brach (Paris: Plon, 1936), p. 242.

[40]*A la recherche du temps perdu (RTP)* (Paris: Bibliothèque de la Pléiade, 1954), t. II, p. 404.

[41]*RTP,* III, pp. 1033-34.

[42]*Monsieur Proust,* p. 446. For the manuscript analysis see André Guyaux, Maurice Paz: "La dissertation de Gisèle" in "Bulletin d'informations proustiennes" (BIP) 11, pp. 35-38.

[43]The quotations are from *Remembrances of Things Past,* II, translated by C. K. Scott Moncrieff (New York: Random House, 1932), 2, pp. 176-79.

[44]Ibid., p. 177.

[45]Ibid., p. 177-78.

[46]Ibid., p. 178.

[47]Ibid., p. 389.

[48]Ibid., p. 178.

[49]Ibid., p. 178.

[50]Ibid., p. 178-79.

[51]Catalogue de l'exposition "Marcel Proust et son temps" (Paris, 1971), n° 146, d), p. 29.

[52]Bibliothèque Nationale, Paris, NAF 16739.

[53]*RTP,* II, p. 733.

2

Trouble and Transparency in Marcel Proust

Roger Shattuck

IT IS TEN MINUTES AFTER NINE O'CLOCK Friday morning in the rundown basement rooms of the Stentor Recording Studios in St. Louis. Sam Gates, fifty, owner and operator of the studio, is seated in front of his equipment threading a reel. Callie Szonic, thirty-five, free-lance radio journalist and producer, is reviewing a script and referring to some books. They are waiting for Henry Fitzhugh, forty-five, professor of philosophy at Columbia University, and for Ned Price, graduate student in French at Washington University in St. Louis. Professor Fitzhugh, known among philosophers for his book on solipsism, has recently published another, *Proust and Perverseness of Thought.* Yesterday he gave a lecture at Washington University sponsored by the philosophy and Romance languages departments. His plane leaves today at noon.

Sound of knocking.

Callie. The door's open. Good morning, Professor Fitzhugh. I'm Callie Szonic. You brought your suitcase! That's fine. We'll have more time to talk before you have to catch your plane. Coffee?

Prof. F. Yes. Thank you.

Callie. This is Sam Gates. Professor Fitzhugh. Sam lets me use his place as my headquarters. I have no office.

Sam. Don't mind me. I have to go out in a few minutes. Why don't you two go into the studio? There's more space and better chairs.

Callie. Thanks, Sam. (*They move to the studio.*)

Prof. F. (*Clearing his throat.*) You can understand, Ms. Szonic, that I need to know a little more about what you're doing before I can decide whether to participate. Your letters say you have funding to do a series of

programs on major authors in world literature. Do you mean to record a
short talk on each author? And who are the authors?

Callie. No, not little lectures. More like conversations. We'll do
an hour on each author. So far we've chosen Faulkner, George Eliot,
Achebe, Goethe, Pascal, Lady Murasaki, and Proust. First a discussion to
place the author in his or her time and describe his or her genius. Then
we'll have readings from the work for the rest of the time. Oral interpretation some people call it. We're hoping National Public Radio will air the
programs. The point is to appeal to a wide audience. It's not a scholarly
undertaking.

Prof. F. I don't understand. Why did you pick me then? My
books are very scholarly, particularly the one on Proust.

Callie. Yes, but you talk about subjects that . . . (*Knock.*) Just a
moment. Come in, Ned.

Ned. Excuse me, excuse me. My car wouldn't start today. Natur-
ally. Professor Fitzhugh? Ned Price. I'm a graduate student in French at
Washington University. Did Callie tell you how we met? In a book store,
where I was reading your book on Proust. She asked me what it's like.
Now she calls me her advisor on Proust. I'm very pleased to meet you.
The reviewers didn't do justice to your Proust book.

Callie. I was just starting to tell Professor F. why we chose *him* to
talk about Proust.

Ned. That's easy. Your chapter on perverseness of thought swept
us away. Also the section on how the overall style of Proust's novel arises
from gossip—malicious, loving, idle, compulsive gossip—the gossip of
someone who cannot bear to let the wheel of words stop turning for fear
that then everything else might disappear. You make your scholarship
pretty lively.

Callie. Ned is an incorrigible Proust enthusiast. Which means he
gossips too. But there's another reason why I invited you to do the Proust
program. We're dealing with an author who took fifteen years to find his
way to the novel and then, after the age of thirty-five, poured everything
into one immense book which he just barely finished in his last fifteen
years. Story of a man obsessed. You know all this better than I do.
Hundreds of characters, complex subplots, hilarious scenes of people's
behavior in social situations, lengthy meditations on the major philosophical
questions of life. In the last stage just before he got started on the *Search*—
incidentally, I agree with you that the old title must go—Proust wrote an

essay on the French romantic author, Gérard de Nerval. It's in *Against Sainte-Beuve*. The essay contains a passage which I've always wanted to hear a Proust scholar comment on. A philosopher more than anyone else. Proust has been talking about . . .

Prof. F. Ms. Szonic, this is beginning to sound like an oral examination. I thought we were going to confer about ways of doing the program.

Callie. Yes, yes. Exactly. I want to know if you think this would make a good lead-in for the discussion. Proust has been discussing *Sylvie,* Nerval's haunting story about three women all of whom the hero loves and loses. The hero is pretty close to Nerval himself speaking in the first person. Proust, who deeply admires Nerval, tells us that everything is colored purple in the story, especially the name Sylvie with its two i-sounds. Rimbaud has the same color for the i-sound in his "Sonnet of the Vowels." Then in one complex and unforgettable sentence—I have it marked right here—Proust states that Nerval's story contains "the mysterious laws of thought which I have often wanted to express—I'd count up to five or six of them." But that's all. Proust doesn't tell us what they are and closes the discussion by saying that there may even be a little too much intelligence in *Sylvie.* Five or six laws of thought—the idea fascinates me. But there's no follow-up. What can we do with the passage?

Prof. F. I've read those pages on Nerval, but I don't remember the specific passage. Five or six laws. . . . There's a challenge for every Proustian alive, philosopher or not. Of course Proust talks about laws all the time. In *Within a Budding Grove* (another title that should be abandoned), the narrator blurts right out that "it's useless to observe people's behavior because you can derive it all from psychological laws." Now, the Nerval passage you quoted doesn't sound ironic or playful. I think Proust gives you the first of his laws right there in the purple i-sounds. He's affirming Baudelaire's *correspondances,* synesthesia, analogies. That law of association of impressions through similarity and proximity leads directly into the great echo chamber of involuntary memory: association in time. How's that for a first law? When you attend to them carefully, things mysteriously connect. The other laws may take a bit longer.

Ned. You make it sound easy. Callie, do you expect Prof. F. to do all the work? No. Then I'll suggest one. This may be more a principle than a law. I mean the double, the Doppelgänger, the identical Other. It doesn't seem to me that Proust necessarily borrowed this device from anyone else—Hoffmann or Poe. It was the natural consequence of his decision to write an autobiographical novel. He lays it right out for us in the Madeleine sequence. The second and third mouthfuls of tea and cake do not fill him again with the original precious essence. Marcel, who at that age may be about half way to becoming the narrator, puts down his cup and turns toward his mind, his spirit, as the source of the essence that surpasses mediocrity and contingency. But—all this is close to verbatim quotation— the mind is in a quandary because "it, the seeking mind, is also the dark countryside where it must do the seeking." The endlessly fruitful dilemma of autobiography consists in the fact that the prey lies *inside* the hunter. Proust enacts this dilemma by making his principal character a double: the narrator and Marcel, seeker and sought, one character at different ages, two virtually identical characters distinguishable only by chronology, by the contingency of time. But style and syntax conspire to blind us to this crucial bifurcation inside the endlessly recurring *I*. Proust's *je* in all its inflections sounds like just one person.

You know what has happened as a result. Almost all Proust critics have become fastidious purists. Since author must never be confused with narrator, the name "Marcel" has virtually disappeared—too close to Proust's name. The editors of the three massive new French editions of the *Search* say "the narrator" for *both* persons of the double. They spurn the name that Proust himself twice tentatively gave to his principal character: Marcel. Yet that name is truly appropriate in a work of fiction displaying a subtle and unmistakable relation to autobiography. In the enacted scenes of this Bildungsroman "the narrator" is a patently inaccurate term to designate a slowly maturing prospective writer one of whose principal traits is, by all the evidence including his own declarations, the incapacity to settle down to write or narrate anything at all. Critics should reconsider their skittishness and return to "Marcel" to refer to the hero and principal character. Even a Kafkaesque "M" for certain roles of Proust's "I" would be better than a blanket "narrator" to cover every aspect of the first person.

Well, I hope I haven't botched my point completely. I see the law of the double as essential to everything Proust wrote. A first person singular tracking itself until . . .

Callie. Ned! I can't let you go on. You agreed not to get off on a rant.

Ned. I'm sorry. I'll try to be quiet.

Prof. F. You must be writing your dissertation on first-person pronouns in Proust. I'm not sure you need *me* here. Now we have two laws out of five. What about you, Ms. Szonic? You should answer your own question. Surely you have an answer.

Callie. Don't forget I'm just a radio journalist. But yes, I may. A couple of pages before the passage about laws in Nerval, Proust describes *Sylvie* as "a dream of a dream" or "a dream within a dream." I feel certain he's alluding to some kind of law. But I can't put my finger on how it works in the *Search*.

Prof. F. In *Aurélia,* another of Nerval's stories, he talks about "the spreading of dream into real life." It's really an analogy for Nerval's incipient insanity. Proust has hidden away in the *Search* far more dreams than we usually remember on first reading. After Albertine is killed in a riding accident, "the *da capo* effect" of Marcel's dreams prevents him from forgetting her, and the narrator describes dreams as "passing intervals of insanity." Proust was never swept away completely by dream or insanity as Nerval was. But the possibility is there always, a law held in abeyance, the threat of the abyss of unreality, of dreams taking over everything.

Callie. You see? I told you a scholar would help me. Now we have three laws: things connect, we are all doubles, and dream encroaches on reality. Where do we go now? More coffee?

Prof. F. Yes, please. You are relentless. I'll try once more. There's a psychological law that applies in many domains of Proust's novel. I wish I had a good name for it. Since I don't, I'll have to borrow a phrase from a critic I have my reservations about, Roger Shattuck. In his second book on Proust, Shattuck himself borrows an expression from Montaigne, *erreur d'âme,* soul error. The term refers to the condition which makes it so difficult for us to cherish what we have and leads us to see mystery and prestige in what we do not possess. Anyone who has read a single volume of Proust can sense the operation of this law in the domain we call romantic love. We say possession is nine tenths of the law. Marcel's extended capture and imprisonment of Albertine demonstrate that in attachments of the heart, possession is one tenth of the law. But soul error, which wants what it does not or cannot have, also explains Proust's rejection of friendship. He presents friendship as a false and distracting personal relationship in which we seek "hospitalization" in another individual instead of cultivating the true life of the mind in ourselves. Shattuck fails to see how essential a role soul error plays in the great driving force of all social relations: snobbery. There's a superb comic page in the second volume about a rich and titled old lady—it's Mme de Villeparisis—arriving at the Grand Hotel in Balbec. All the guests in the dining room are consumed with curiosity about her and the desire to make her acquaintance—a desire they then half-successfully suppress by convincing themselves that she is ugly and not worth knowing. Proust has written a subtle modern version of Æsop's fable of the sour grapes. All these constantly readjusted states of mind turn on the axis of soul error. Of course now we have come back around to what I discuss in my chapter on "perverseness of mind" in Proust. I cannot judge whether soul error has equal sway in Nerval, an author I don't know as well as the two of you.

Ned. Yes. Yes. Everything in *Sylvie* and *Aurélia* depends on keeping the ideal at a distance in order to sustain the illusion and the emotion. But . . . going through a set of laws like this. . . . If I can remember accurately. . . . Just a minute. Borges. That's who it is. Somewhere I read about Borges stating in a lecture the principles of fantastic art. They are almost the same ones that we have pulled out of Proust and Nerval. I think I can remember Borges's four devices. The work within the work, the contamination of reality by dream or unreality, the voyage in time, and the double. The voyage in time may be Borges's version of memory and association. But what does it all mean? Should we believe that these are four great universals of all thinking and all art? I'm not sure I want to be told that there are just so many laws that cover all cases.

Callie. They're not so different from one another if you look carefully. I think there may be an almost infinite number of laws of this kind all representing one principle: *interference.* The interference of one domain with another, one sense with another, one time with another, one place with another, one state of mind with another, one social level with another, and so on. Proust blurs everything, all our classifications, even our sense of character. Still, the *Search* represents a deep and strong faith in something—in the life of the mind, I suppose.

Prof. F. Perhaps you can group all the laws so far under the heading of interference. But there's at least one more major law that does not belong with the rest. I think of it as the principle of self-determination. At three different stages in his career—in 1904 writing about Ruskin, in 1908 writing on Sainte-Beuve, and then some ten years later quoting Elstir in his studio—Proust states his conviction that "we cannot receive the truth from anyone; we have to create it for ourselves." Here we have the opposite of interference. In another place he describes every writer as having to start out from scratch, like Homer. Each time Proust seems to be reaffirming that ontogeny recapitulates phylogeny—not just in the embryo but in life itself. He had his own monadology.

Ned. Isn't this what all the critics refer to as radical subjectivity? the impossibility of true communication between human beings? All the extended social occasions in the *Search,* which is full of them, and all the scenes driven by some form of appetite or love for another person, describe only the most superficial form of exchange between individuals. As you write yourself, gossip drives out all other forms of exchange. Marcel cannot even kiss Albertine properly because her face gets in the way. And in the opening scenes of "Combray," Marcel and his mother cannot converse easily with one another, even alone. Her goodness and tenderness reach him, unalloyed, only when she begins reading George Sand aloud to him in a voice whose lack of affectation expresses true "moral distinction." But there is a yawning dilemma here. If we must learn everything for and by ourselves, if we cannot communicate essential truths to one another, why write books? Why read them? Isn't literature a hoax exposed in the very pages we are reading?

Callie. And why are you in graduate school scrutinizing these contradictions and digging yourself into an intellectual hole?

Prof. F. That may be what graduate school is for. But now you two are going to have to let me talk about what's on my mind instead of asking me questions as if this were an interview or an examination. After receiving your letters, Ms. Szonic, I tried to . . .

Callie. Please forgive me, Professor Fitzhugh. We've been impolite. What are your ideas for the program?

Prof. F. No need to apologize. A discussion like this accomplishes more than a monologue. Ned just said the word I have on my mind. Reading. Are you aware how many scholars and critics have published about reading in Proust? At least two full-length books and scores of articles in French, English, German, Japanese, and other languages. It's true that one of the essential subjects of the *Search* is reading and writing. But most of the criticism I've read leaves me deeply dissatisfied. One of the most carefully written scenes in the novel concerns Marcel reading in the garden in Combray. It comes near the opening; any reader of Proust should know it. Marcel is persuaded by his grandmother to leave his bedroom where darkness, stray rays of light, street sounds, and other distractions prevent him from reading. With an unidentified book he takes shelter in the depths of a canopied cane-and-canvas chair under a chestnut tree in the garden. Here Marcel is solitary and hidden enough to read. The narrator devotes five pages to describing and narrating the act of reading a fictional work. I see you have the English translation of the *Search* there. Pass me the opening volume, would you.

The narrator moves in four carefully distinguished steps from the innermost recesses of Marcel's consciousness to the real world outside that surrounds him. Remember? First comes the striking metaphor of an incandescent object. It evaporates anything in its path and therefore can never touch a substance it approaches. The scene starts with a version of our last fundamental law: the incapacity of the consciousness to make contact with any other consciousness. "A narrow spiritual border" always separates us from the real world of other beings and other things. But: one precious mental activity can transcend this limit, this law. Reading. Proust explains this everyday miracle by examining the next level of Marcel's mind. While he reads, Marcel's consciousness is released by his *croyance,* his "belief in the philosophical richness and the beauty of the book." And the book offers a very special kind of material for his emotions to deal with. The novelist sets before us not the material opaqueness of real beings but transparent images evoked by words, images "which our soul can assimilate," which our consciousness can make contact with. These immaterial images have the further advantage of not being subject to contingent human time. They can move at an accelerated speed that reveals changes we fail to notice at the pace of ordinary living. The novelist's images have the privileged status of a prolonged, clarified dream.

The third level of phenomena described by the narrator in Marcel's mental state of reading consists of the imaginary landscape in which the imaginary characters move, a countryside that seems to belong to "true Nature" with a capital N, Nature "worthy of being studied and explored." And here the narrator or Proust places a paragraph that sets the tone for the rest of the book, its essential action and its intellectual life. Let me read the paragraph. There's no other way to convey the pace and the rhythm of Proust's style. The prison image in the second sentence recasts the earlier image of an incandescent filament that cannot make contact with anything. And notice how insistently he uses the word *soul.* I've checked; it's in the original. *Ame* means our entire mental, emotional, and spiritual equipment. The passage describes how an irresistible force—later Proust calls it "that immense desire to know life"—meets an immovable object—the inaccessability of material, opaque beings. Just listen. I'll go slowly. It's less than a page.

> Had my parents allowed me, when I read a book, to pay a visit to the region it described, I should have felt that I was making an enormous advance towards the ultimate conquest of truth. For even if we have the sensation of being always enveloped in, surrounded by our own soul, still it does not seem a fixed and immovable prison; rather do we seem to be borne away with it, and perpetually struggling to transcend it, to break out into the world, with a perpetual discouragement as we hear endlessly all around us that unvarying sound which is not an echo from without, but the resonance of a vibration from within. We try to discover in things, which become precious to us on that account, the reflection of what our soul has projected on to them; we are disillusioned when we find that in this natural state, they are devoid of the charm which they owed, in our minds, to the association of certain ideas; sometimes we mobilise all the forces of that soul in a glittering array in order to bring our influence to bear on other human beings who, we very well know, are situated outside ourselves where we can never reach them. And so, if I always imagined the woman I loved in the setting I most longed at the time to visit, if I wished that it were she who would show it to me, who would open to me the gates of an unknown world, it was not a mere chance association of thoughts; no, it was because my dreams of travel and of love were only moments—which I isolate artificially today as though I were cutting sections at different heights in the jet of a fountain, iridescent but seemingly without flow or motion—moments in a single, undeviating, irresistible outpouring of all the forces of my life.

What can I say about such a passage? There's nothing to add. Yet one could talk endlessly about how much philosophy, how much feeling, is packed into every sentence. We want most to know precisely what we cannot know—the universe of beings that lies outside us. Our soul pours itself out by a kind of fate—entirely in vain. We live a tragi-comic paradox. Near the end of the passage you can hear the narrator, "moments . . . which I isolate artificially today," speaking in the present tense, separating himself from Marcel in the past and cozying up to Proust in the present writing this book, these words.   The narrative goes on to . . . What is it, Ned? You want to say something?

Ned. Is it that obvious? Yes, just a parenthesis about the fountain analogy. I've thought a lot about it. The fountain belongs to a special set of images that affirm both flux and stasis. There aren't many. Heraclitus's river, the one you cannot step into twice. In our time, Wordsworth's "standing waterfalls" and Pater's "candle flame." Each one a streaming stillness. Proust's whole paragraph echoes Heraclitus's balance of opposites.

Prof. F. You're right. I never thought of that link. Well, the fourth stage of Marcel's reading is the immediate, Sunday afternoon world of a chair sheltered in the silent garden. At regular yet unpredictable intervals that hushed scene is invaded by the notes striking the hour from the Saint-Hilaire bell tower. This outer layer of familiar circumstances contains the other layers going back to Marcel's soul or consciousness. They form a kind of multiple capsule or monad. Now all kinds of images in these five pages on reading tell how cut off Marcel remains from the real world he yearns desperately to reach, to touch. Yet the last significant substantive of the scene is *crystal,* reinforced by the adjective *limpid.* These two words characterize the magical, transparent hours of reading, our closest approach to communication, to getting out of ourselves.

Ned. What you say about the transparency we find through reading makes me think of another word Proust uses from time to time to describe the ordinary state of life without transparency. The word in French is *trouble,* which doesn't mean "trouble" the way we use it in English. It means a troubled, a disturbed, a confused state of mind. I began to keep a list. Toward the end of the *Search* the pages Marcel reads from the Goncourt journal cause a *"trouble"* in his mind because they seem to describe transparently people he has himself known and never grasped so clearly in life. If reading is our crystal ball, we live in a state of *trouble*—cloudiness, uncertainty.

Callie. You said earlier, Professor Fitzhugh, that you are dissatisfied by what the critics have written about reading? Why is that? Whom do you mean?

Prof. F. (*Looking at his watch.*) I think the cab I ordered may be here now. I'll have to be brief. There's one critic who seems to have led most of the others in the wrong direction. Do you know Paul de Man's essay on Proust in *Allegories of Reading?* He spends half his time discussing metaphor and metonymy in the two paragraphs just *before* the garden reading scene—paragraphs in which Marcel essentially fails to read. Then he quotes at length from the paragraph I just read and examines what he calls a "reversal." Consciousness is captive within us, yet it chooses "to submit itself to the test of truth" in the outside world. De Man says that Proust's novel leaves no doubt that the test must fail, and that this failure is affirmed right here "in a passage whose thematic and rhetorical strategy it reduces to naught." Proust's passage never attains the desired "totalization" or synthesis. Now, de Man's Hegelian vocabulary is difficult enough to follow. But the principal flaw is that de Man has read the passage wrong. The narrator—here very close to Proust—is not trying to synthesize or "totalize" anything. He is presenting a contrast, an opposition between *real life,* in which our attempts to communicate with other beings are inevitably thwarted, and the special activity of *reading,* relying on transparent images, which permits a closer approach to the conquest of truth, to knowledge. Far from deconstructing itself by an inner contradiction or a failure to "totalize," this passage presents the special rewards of reading as an activity complementary to living, not replacing it but opening up its potential spaces. The earlier lessons about reading from "Journées de lecture" hover close by. Although time spent reading is "fully lived," it brings us only to the threshold of spiritual life, provides incitements to it. De Man fails to take account of the close symbiotic relation Proust describes between reading and living.

There's one more step. As a philosopher I have to take it, even at my peril. Near the beginning of these pages on reading, the narrator speaks of Marcel's "belief" in the philosophic richness and the beauty of the book he is reading. Belief. It may be the key to everything. At the end of "Combray," the narrator undertakes to explain why the two "ways"— Swann's Way and Guermantes's Way—have provided the essential structure and the most significant episodes of his intellectual life. Belief, a child's belief in the beings and things he lives among, lends them unforgettable reality and meaning. A kind of transparency without *trouble.* The child's belief in his world corresponds to the belief that we can provisionally reassemble and direct toward the book we are reading. In the *Search,* Proust casts doubt on many of our treasured values—love, friendship, social attainment, idolatrous forms of art. Beneath it all remains a startlingly invincible *faith*—faith in childhood experience and in reading.

Sam. (*He had come in and waited during the last sentences.*) Sorry to interrupt. The cab driver out front says he's come for you, Professor.

Callie. How did it go? Did you get it all?

Sam. Perfect. This is one of the best tapes yet. You have a pretty good voice for radio, Professor. I could even follow a lot of what you said. And I've never read a word of Proust—Prowst I probably would have said. Maybe I'll have a look at his book.

Prof. F. (*Incredulous, a little peeved.*) You mean you recorded all this? (*To Callie.*) You said we were going to plan a program. I never agreed. . .

Callie. Don't worry, Professor Fitzhugh. We taped some great material this morning. In a formal interview, thinking about how they sound, people often freeze up. You were fine. Believe me. And I promise you, nothing will leave this studio without your permission. We'll clean up the tape a little, make a few cuts, and send you a cassette copy. Then you'll tell us what you think. If you insist, we can do it over, or parts of it. But wait till you hear what we send you. You even did a reading for us!

Prof. F. I'll be damned. Does everyone walk into your trap as innocently as I did? All right, I'll wait to hear the results.

References

Proust, Marcel. *A la recherche du temps perdu.* Bibliothèque de la Pléiade, 3 vols., Paris: Gallimard, 1954.

Proust, Marcel. *Contre Sainte-Beuve.* Bibliothèque de la Pléiade, Paris: Gallimard, 1971.

Borges, Jorge Luis. *Labyrinths.* New York: New Directions, 1962. Introduction by James E. Irby, p. xviii.

De Man, Paul. "Reading (Proust)" in *Allegories of Reading.* New Haven: Yale University Press, 1979.

Shattuck, Roger. *Marcel Proust.* Princeton: Princeton University Press, 1974.

Specific references within the text are as follows:

Page 19, lines 16-18: *CSB* 239
Page 19, lines 26-27: I 513
Page 20, lines 8-9: I 45
Page 21, line 7: *CSB* 237
Page 21, line 14: III 538
Page 21, lines 15-16: III 540
Page 21, line 36: II 394
Page 22, lines 1-6: I 678
Page 22, lines 37-38: *CSB* 177; see also *CSB* 220 and I 864
Page 23, line 15: I 42
Page 24, lines 17-18: I 84
Page 24, line 21: I 85
Page 24, line 30: I 86
Page 25, line 1: III 553
Page 25, lines 34-35: I 87; I 93-94
Page 27, lines 4-5: 71
Page 27, lines 7-8: 71
Page 27, line 20: *CSB* 160
Page 27, line 30: I 184

3

La Réception d'*A la recherche du temps perdu* aux Etats-Unis

Elyane Dezon-Jones

ALORS QUE L'ON POSSEDE de nombreux renseignements sur l'accueil que la critique anglaise a réservé à l'œuvre de Marcel Proust, dès la publication des premiers volumes d'*A la recherche du temps perdu* puisque le tout premier compte-rendu de *Du côté de chez Swann* rédigé en anglais par Mary Robinson Duclaux, parut dans le *Times Literary Supplement* du 4 décembre 1913, la manière dont le livre fut reçu aux Etats-Unis est plus difficile à cerner à cause d'un ensemble de facteurs socio-culturels qui ont obscurci les différences entre les réactions de la critique américaine et celles de la critique anglaise. Cet état de choses s'explique d'abord par le fait que des deux côtés de l'Atlantique, on utilise la langue anglaise comme véhicule critique, ce qui entretient une confusion inhérente à toute étude utilisant l'adjectif "anglo-saxon," que ce soit l'article de Gérard Tougas "Marcel Proust devant la critique anglo-saxonne," qui parut dans la *Revue de Littérature comparée* de janvier-mars 1956, ou bien le récent panorama proposé par R. Gibson "Proust et la critique anglo-saxonne," publié dans les *Cahiers Marcel Proust 11, Etudes proustiennes IV*, en 1982.

Selon Gérard Tougas, "il y eut un décalage entre la réputation littéraire de Marcel Proust, dont les origines remontent à 1919 en France (Prix Goncourt) et qui se fit en Angleterre presque simultanément" et la réception de l'œuvre en Amérique: "Il semble bien que ce soit principalement sous l'influence du courant d'opinion anglais admirablement secondé par la traduction de Scott Moncrieff, que l'Amérique s'est mise à la lecture de Proust. [. . .] Entre la culture française et le nouveau monde, l'Angleterre servait de trait d'union."[1]

On retrouve la même idée chez Albert Salvan, qui écrit dans son article "Proust devant l'opinion américaine" dans les *Cahiers de l'Association Internationale des Etudes Françaises* du 12 juin 1960, que "les critiques anglais ont servi d'intercesseurs." Cette interprétation néglige plusieurs points, dont le premier concerne la polémique autour de la traduction de *la Recherche,* entreprise par C. K. Scott Moncrieff, sans l'accord préalable de Proust, qui "lui-même avait songé à Gilbert Cannan, traducteur du *Jean-Christophe* de Romain Rolland."[2] Il y eut un malentendu initial sur la traduction des titres car Proust, alerté par Violet et Sydney Schiff, pensa que *Swann's Way* voulait dire "à la manière de Swann" et écrivit à Gaston Gallimard: "Je tiens à mon œuvre, que je ne laisserai pas des Anglais démolir."[3]

Si le titre générique choisi par C. K. Scott Moncrieff pour servir d'équivalence plutôt que de traduction à *A la recherche du temps perdu: Remembrance of Things Past,* pouvait évoquer immédiatement un vers du trentième sonnet de Shakespeare pour un public anglais cultivé, la référence n'était nullement transparente pour les lecteurs d'outre-Atlantique. Le 21 septembre 1921, un compte-rendu du *Swann* de Scott Moncrieff parut dans le *Times Literary Supplement* et donna le ton à toute une série d'articles qui suivirent et s'accordèrent pour trouver que cette version, publiée à Londres par Chatto et Windus, était meilleure que l'original.

Contrairement à ce qu'on croit, il n'y eut pas un décalage de dix ans entre la publication de l'œuvre de Proust en traduction en Angleterre et en Amérique mais seulement d'une année. En effet *Swann's Way* paraît à New York, chez Holt en 1922 et les comptes rendus qui paraissent dans les journaux américains sont généralement favorables. Ainsi Joseph Collins écrit dans le *New York Times* du 26 novembre 1922: "M. Proust est un créateur de grande littérature, un maître de style extraordinaire, qui a une profonde connaissance du cœur et de l'esprit humains."

Les droits de publication sont rachetés l'année suivante par Thomas Seltzer qui fait paraître en 1924 *A l'ombre des jeunes filles en fleurs* (*Within a Budding Grove* dans la traduction de Scott Moncrieff) puis en 1925 *Le Côté de Guermantes* (*The Guermantes Way*). Dans les deux cas la qualité de la traduction est mise en question. Ainsi dans la *Saturday Review of Literature* du 4 juillet 1925, O. H. Dunbar reproche le fait que "dans les passages simples, la traduction devient mécanique et les mots sont rendus en anglais le plus simple sans tenir compte des expressions idiomatiques." Thomas Seltzer revend alors les droits à un autre éditeur américain, Boni, qui publiera les autres volumes de *la Recherche* dans l'ordre suivant:

Sodome et Gomorrhe (*Cities of the Plain*) en 1928, qui aura un accueil critique mitigé et un succès de scandale, *La Prisonnière* (*The Captive*) en 1930 et *Albertine disparue* (*The Sweet Cheat Gone*) en 1931, à propos duquel Edgar Johnson fait remarquer dans le *New York Evening Post* du 10 mars que ce "volume révèle en divers endroits le fait que Proust n'a pas eu le temps de finir de réviser. . . . Mais la structure architecturale est là et bien là." Et enfin *Le Temps retrouvé* (*The Past Recaptured*) paraît en 1932, dans la traduction de Frederick A. Blossom qui fut bien accueillie au départ puisque Angel Flores écrit dans le *New York Herald Tribune Books* le 28 août 1932:

> *Le Temps retrouvé* n'est pas seulement le finale nécessaire, le dénouement des événements, la conclusion de l'action—c'est véritablement la meilleure explication du Proustisme—un discours de la méthode. . . . Les six premières parties d'*A la recherche du temps perdu* furent données au lecteur anglais par le défunt C. K. Moncrieff, maître en l'art de la traduction. Après sa mort, bien des mains habiles se sont essayé à achever la difficile entreprise, qui, réussie en Angleterre par Stephen Hudson, vient d'être brillamment surpassée par le Docteur Frederick A. Blossom.

Ceci ne fut pas l'avis de tout le monde. Le livre de Proust avait changé d'éditeur trois fois, aux Etats-Unis, entre 1922 et 1932. Les droits de publication de la traduction furent acquis par Random House, qui en fit une première édition, en quatre volumes, en 1934 et en proposa une nouvelle, en 1981, dans une version révisée par Terence Kilmartin, qui s'appuie sur les traductions de Scott Moncrieff et le texte établi par P. Clarac et A. Ferré pour les éditions Gallimard dans la collection de la Bibliothèque de la Pléiade, en 1954.

Il faut faire un sort à part au *Temps retrouvé*. On sait que sous le pseudonyme de Stephen Hudson, Sydney Schiff traduisit le dernier volume de *la Recherche* après la mort de Scott Moncrieff en 1930, sous le titre *Time Regained*. Cependant, si l'on en croit Bennett Cerf, directeur de Random House à l'époque:

> Comme son prédécesseur (Thomas Seltzer) notre édition utilisa la célèbre traduction de C. K. Scott Moncrieff, qui mourut avant de pouvoir achever la septième partie, *Le Temps retrouvé*. Ceci fut traduit par Frederick Blossom, et pour une raison quelconque, Alexander

Woolcroft s'en offensa vivement et écrivit un compte-rendu mordant dans le *New Yorker.* Il fut ainsi à l'origine d'une controverse qui dura quelque temps, avec d'autres critiques prenant le parti de Blossom, qui les rejoignit dans leurs attaques contre Woolcott—lui-même ayant bien sûr d'autres remarques à ajouter. Inutile de dire que tout ce débat ne fut pas mauvais pour nos ventes et que Proust se vendit dans notre beau coffret, comme jamais auparavant.[4]

En fait *Le Temps retrouvé* fut traduit une troisième fois par Andreas Mayor en 1970, pour Chatto et Windus, en gardant le titre qu'avait préféré Frederick Blossom, *The Past Recaptured,* en 1932 et également conservé par Terence Kilmartin en 1981.

S'il y a médiation anglaise entre l'œuvre de Proust et les lecteurs américains, il paraît qu'elle s'effectue au niveau même de la traduction du texte original, en une autre langue, l'anglais, qui a ses différences d'avec l'américain. Mais les premiers lecteurs de l'édition Seltzer, prévue en sept volumes, ou Random House en quatre volumes à partir de 1934, étaient habitués à lire les œuvres européennes traduites en anglais britannique et selon Albert Schinz qui a étudié le sort du livre français aux Etats-Unis entre 1914 et 1936, "on lit autant en Amérique qu'en Europe, grâce surtout à l'énorme développement des bibliothèques publiques"; grâce aussi aux nombreuses traductions, une étude plus poussée des langues étrangères dans le cadre scolaire et surtout à

ces innombrables clubs de dames [. . . .] quand on ne parle pas politique, soviétisme, dettes de guerre, c'est la littérature française qui est le plus souvent à l'honneur: à défaut d'orateurs compétents ces dames n'hésitent pas à discuter elles-mêmes de Baudelaire ou de Rimbaud, de Marcel Proust ou d'André Gide.[5]

En réalité, ce sont les écrivains et les journalistes américains résidant à Paris entre 1920 et 1930 qui furent les premiers véritables médiateurs de l'œuvre proustienne, parce qu'ils eurent accès au texte original d'*A la recherche du temps perdu,* dont la publication s'échelonna de 1913 à 1927. C'est dans une revue américaine et non pas anglaise que parut le premier fragment traduit en anglais extrait d'*A la recherche:* "Saint-Loup: a Portrait" fut publié dans le numéro d'octobre 1920 du *Dial,* accompagné d'une critique élogieuse de Richard Aldington: "The Approach to M.

Marcel Proust." La même année, le magazine anglais *Land and Water* refusa de publier les passages du *Côté de chez Swann* que proposait C. K. Scott Moncrieff. Sous la direction de Scofield Thayer et de Sibley Watson, *The Dial* fit paraître deux autres articles favorables à Proust: "A Monument to Proust" par Malcolm Cowley en mars 1923 et "Marcel Proust: A Prophet of Despair," plus nuancé, par Francis Birrell dans le numéro de mai 1923. En octobre 1924, Ernest Hemingway publia dans *Der Querschnitt* un poème qui avait pour but de critiquer les positions critiques du *Dial* et de régler des comptes personnels:

> Vous avez tous été des enfants qui ont réussi.
> Maintenant nettoyons le gachis.
> Le Cadran élève un monument à Proust.
> Nous avons élevé un monument à Ezra.
> Un monument est un monument.
> Après tout c'est l'esprit de la chose qui compte.[6]

Hemingway parodie ici le style de Gertrude Stein et prend la défense d'Ezra Pound, qui fréquentait le 20 rue Jacob où résidait Natalie Clifford Barney, à qui Proust rendit lui-même visite en novembre 1921, après avoir reçu un exemplaire de ses *Pensées d'une Amazone,* portant la dédicace suivante: "A Monsieur Marcel Proust, dont la compréhension mérite cet exemplaire non expurgé," après surtout une année d'échanges épistolaires sur les questions de *Sodome et Gomorrhe.* Cependant le jugement final de Natalie Clifford Barney sur le traitement de Gomorrhe par Proust est loin d'être favorable; selon George D. Painter, "quand Miss Barney lut ses derniers volumes, elle trouva qu'Albertine et ses amies n'étaient pas charmantes mais surtout invraisemblables; elle déclara sèchement: N'enfreint pas qui veut ces mystères d'Eleusis."[7]

La même démarche se retrouve chez Ezra Pound, qui avait établi dans le numéro 71 du *Dial* d'octobre 1921 un intéressant parallèle entre la satire du monde telle qu'on la trouve chez Henry James et ce qu'on peut en lire dans *Guermantes* mais qui traita Proust de "petit lèche-bottes" et lui reprocha de "croire vraiment que ses maquereaux, ses pédérastes et ses imbéciles opulents étaient *importants*" dans une lettre de 1933 à William Shepard. Comme Hemingway, Ezra Pound fréquentait aussi la rue de Fleurus où habitait Gertrude Stein, qui fut une des premières à comprendre la radicale nouveauté de la méthode expérimentale que Proust appliquait au roman, puisqu'elle le mit au premier rang, avec Joyce et elle-même, en écrivant dans *Portraits and Repetitions:*

> une chose que vous savez tous, c'est que dans les trois romans écrits au cours de cette génération, qui sont les choses importantes écrites au cours de cette génération, il n'y a dans aucun d'eux d'histoire. Il n'y en a pas dans Proust, dans *The Making of Americans,* ni dans *Ulysse.*[8]

Tous les écrivains américains qui séjournent en France après la première guerre mondiale entendent discuter de Proust dans les cercles réduits qu'ils fréquentent, surtout après l'attribution du Prix Goncourt à *A l'ombre des jeunes filles en fleurs* en 1919. Au contraire de ce que dit Gérard Tougas lorsqu'il fait état du silence des agences de presse américaines établies en Europe sur la mort de Marcel Proust le 18 novembre 1922, Ford Madox Ford décrit l'effet produit par cet événement dans les milieux anglophones parisiens comme tenant de la catastrophe internationale dans son recueil de souvenirs intitulé: *It Was the Nightingale,* publié à Philadelphie en 1933.

La réaction de la critique anglaise à la disparition de Proust fut de constituer un recueil d'articles édités par C. K. Scott Moncrieff, *Marcel Proust: An English Tribute* en 1923. La réaction américaine fut plus diffuse, plus lente et plus complexe car elle affecta directement les romanciers américains qui se posèrent sous des formes diverses la question formulée par Virginia Woolf dans une lettre du 3 octobre 1922 à Roger Fry: "Qu'est-ce qui reste à écrire après cela?"[9]

De Sherwood Anderson à Jack Kerouac, en passant par Francis Scott Fitzgerald, William Faulkner et Thomas Wolfe, les romanciers américains de l'entre-deux-guerres vont traiter à leur manière le thème proustien, la recherche du temps perdu, l'œuvre de Proust constituant, comme l'a si bien dit Thibaudet "une cellule-mère" pour toute une génération d'écrivains, à commencer par celle à laquelle Gertrude Stein avait appliqué un adjectif proustien par excellence: "perdue," et dont le représentant le plus illustre est peut-être l'auteur du *Great Gatsby,* qu'Hemingway présenta à Gertrude Stein en 1925, année de la publication du roman.

Dans le *Great Gatsby,* en effet, F. Scott Fitzgerald reprend systématiquement la thématique de la recherche du temps perdu, en manipulant les voix narratives au point de faire parfois entendre au lecteur des échos de Proust. Pour ne citer qu'un exemple, il suffit de comparer le passage au cours duquel Nick Carraway, le narrateur fitzgeraldien, écrit: "il était neuf heures—presque aussitôt après je regardai ma montre et découvris qu'il était dix heures,"[10] avec celui de la *Recherche* où Marcel en train de lire au jardin fait la même expérience: "et à chaque heure, il me semblait que c'était quelques instants auparavant seulement que la précédente avait sonné."[11] Le roman de Fitzgerald s'organise autour de la quête de Gatsby qui veut retrouver le passé perdu sous la forme d'une fugitive qui s'appelle non pas Albertine mais Daisy Buchanan. A Nick Carraway qui l'avertit des dangers de son entreprise et lui affirme: "On ne peut pas retrouver le temps perdu," Gatsby répond sur un ton incrédule: "Pas retrouver le temps perdu [. . .] Mais si, bien sûr qu'on le peut."[12]

The Great Gatsby présente les récits d'une triple recherche du temps perdu: celle du héros éponyme, celle du narrateur et celle de l'auteur qui se penche sur le passé de l'Amérique. Son auteur admirait la traduction que Scott Moncrieff avait faite du roman de Proust, puisque dans une lettre à sa fille datée du 11 mars 1939, il écrit: "Tu n'as pas tout à fait raison pour les traductions (la poésie, bien sûr, ne peut pas être traduite, mais il y a des exceptions, comme le Rubaiyat). Les traductions du russe de Constance Garnett sont excellentes et celle de Proust par Scott Moncrieff est un chef-d'œuvre en soi."[13]

En 1925 également, William Faulkner passa quelques semaines à Paris, rue Servandonni, mais il avait déjà entendu parler de Proust par Sherwood Anderson, à qui il venait de rendre visite à la Nouvelle-Orléans et qui avait fait un voyage en France en 1921. Dans le catalogue qu'il dresse des livres que contient la bibliothèque personnelle de William Faulkner dans sa maison de Rowan Oak, à Oxford, Mississippi, Joseph Blotner fait état d'une édition Gallimard de 1919 *Un amour de Swann,* aux côtés la traduc-tion de Scott Moncrieff dans l'édition Random House de 1934. En réalité l'édition d'*Un amour de Swann* ne date pas de 1919 mais de 1932. Cependant Faulkner lui-même a reconnu des influences françaises sur sa formation d'écrivain, dans une interview qu'il a accordée à Loic Bouvard le 30 novembre 1952: "J'ai été influencé par Flaubert et par Balzac . . . Et par Bergson, évidemment. Après avoir lu *A la recherche du temps perdu,* j'ai dit: c'est ça et j'ai souhaité l'avoir écrit moi-même."[14] La recherche du temps perdu semble être chez Faulkner une méthode d'écriture qui universa-lise l'appréhension humaine du flux temporel et Jean Pouillon a raison de souligner que "comme celui de Proust, le passé de Faulkner n'est pas seule-ment son passé mais le passé du monde."[15] En ayant systématiquement recours au retour en arrière, aux expériences de mémoire involontaire et au démantèlement de la chronologie à l'intérieur du récit des romans du Yoknapatawpha County, Faulkner pousse la technique proustienne jusqu'au point de rupture et se fera accuser de trucage par divers critiques alors que d'autres feront des rapprochements immédiats avec le traitement du temps romanesque par Proust. Ainsi, R. P. Adams croit fermement que Faulkner a fait son apprentissage en lisant Proust: *"Le Bruit et la Fureur,* de même que la plupart des autres œuvres de Faulkner qui connurent un succès retentissant, révèle les mêmes préoccupations obsessionnelles du temps, de la mémoire et du changement qu'*A la recherche du temps perdu.* Sans doute Faulkner trouva-t-il dans les expériences précédentes de Proust ce qu'il apprit des techniques qu'il utilisa fort habilement pour traiter ces questions."[16]

Faulkner confirme cette hypothèse mais en réduit la portée lorsqu'il déclare en 1956: "Quand j'ai lu Joyce et Proust il est possible que ma carrière d'écrivain ait été déjà fixée, de sorte qu'elle ne pouvait pas être influencée autrement que dans les ficelles du métier, pour ainsi dire."[17]

"Les ficelles du métier" de romancier, c'est chez Proust avant tout autre que les trouvera Thomas Wolfe, ainsi que le démontre Paul Delakas dans le chapitre V de son livre intitulé *Thomas Wolfe et les écrivains français de son temps.* Maladivement obsédé par la fuite du temps, Thomas Wolfe se met à lire *la Recherche* dans le texte en 1925, comme en témoigne sa correspondance. En 1929, il écrit à Henry T. Volkening qu'il est toujours plongé dans les délices et les difficultés d'une lecture intensive de Proust. Et on peut dater avec certitude de février 1925 le passage de *Of Time and the River (Du Temps et du Fleuve)* où Eugene Gant, le héros du livre, introduit dans la bibliothèque de Mathilde de Mornaye "lui posa quelques questions sur les écrivains français modernes, Proust, Gide, Romains et Cocteau entre autres." Enfin, dans une lettre qu'il envoie le 29 juillet 1937 à Elizabeth Nowell, Thomas Wolfe parle des qualités proustiennes de sa prose:

> mon but quand j'aurai fini (la soirée chez Jack), est d'avoir une section complète de l'ordre social, une sorte de tapisserie dense et étroitement tissée faite des vies et des pensées et des destinées de trente ou quarante personnes, et toutes incarnées dans la structure de l'histoire. C'est d'un dessein élaboré; ça doit l'être; c'est, je suppose quelque peu proustien, mais ça aussi, ça doit l'être. . .[18]

Le bloc romanesque formé par la tétralogie *Look Homeward, Angel* (1929) (*Que l'Ange regarde de ce côté*), *Of Time and the River* (1935) (*Du Temps et du Fleuve*) et des deux volumes publiés après la mort de Thomas Wolfe en 1938 et édités par Maxwell Perkins: *The Web and the Rock* (1939) (*La Toile et le Roc*) et *You Can't Go Home Again* (1940) fut tout de suite placé dans la tradition de Proust par la critique américaine. En 1936, Mary M. Colum affirme que "comme Proust, Wolfe nous raconte sa lutte avec les éléments du Temps."[19] Et en 1941, Joseph Warren Beach, dans son étude sur le roman américain entre 1920 et 1930, reconnaît entre Proust et Thomas Wolfe une communauté d'expérience psychologique au niveau de l'appréhension et de la transcription des phénomènes temporels "qu'on trouve dans l'évocation au moyen de sensations présentes ou d'impressions presque identiques perçues dans la tendre enfance." Et en effet, il y a de multiples scènes de réminiscences proustiennes dans les romans de Thomas Wolfe, dont nous ne donnerons qu'un exemple pertinent: au grelot de la porte du jardin de la maison de Tante Léonie qui résonne dans la mémoire du narrateur de *la Recherche* et l'incite à se mettre à l'œuvre pour inscrire dans l'écriture et fixer dans le temps son "tintement criard, ferrugineux et glacé," correspond la cloche qu'Eugène Gant entend sonner dans *Look Homeward, Angel,* dont le titre initial était *O Lost* (O Perdu): "comme il écoutait, le fantôme du souvenir lui traversa la mémoire et il crut avoir un instant retrouvé ce qu'il avait perdu."[20]

Il faut noter que les critiques qui abordent la question du temps dans l'œuvre si vaste de Thomas Wolfe associent toujours son nom à celui de Proust, formant un corpus indirect de critique proustienne, de critique au second degré pourrait-on dire, qui classe Proust sous l'étiquette de "romancier du temps," comme l'avait fait Percy Wyndham Lewis dans son ouvrage *Time and Western Man* en 1927, où dans les quelques pages qu'il consacre à Proust, il lui reproche de "s'embaumer vivant."

S'il est vrai que "le héros de *Look Homeward, Angel* a des affinités avec le Jay Gatsby de Fitzgerald et le Quentin Compson dans *The Sound and the Fury* de William Faulkner," comme le note T. G. Moser, c'est parce que ces trois personnages "descendent" directement du Marcel de *la Recherche*. Et on va attaquer leurs auteurs sur ce point. Il semble, en effet, qu'un changement d'attitude se soit produit à la fin des années quarante et que l'intérêt soulevé par le thème de la recherche du temps perdu, lancé par Marcel Proust et repris par les romanciers américains majeurs de l'entre-deux-guerres, ait commencé à décliner avec la parution d'un article de W.

Frohock qui parut dans la *Southwest Review* en 1948: "Of Time and Neurosis" ("Du temps et de la névrose") qui commence ainsi: "il est paradoxal de constater qu'une nation qui a une histoire aussi brève que la nôtre soit aussi obsédée que nous le sommes par la fuite du temps."

L'ultime métamorphose de la thématique de la recherche du temps perdu sera sa spatialisation dans le roman de Jack Kerouac: *On the Road* (*Sur la route*) en 1957. Le héros, Dean Moriarty, dont le narrateur, Sal Paradise raconte l'histoire, ne se sépare jamais d'un des tomes du livre de Proust. A la fin du roman, Sal reconnaît la présence de Dean Moriarty parce qu'il voit d'abord "un livre abîmé posé sur le poste de radio, le Proust de Dean" qui est utilisé comme un signe annonciateur, un symbole de reconnaissance entre le narrateur/auteur Sal et son personnage Dean Moriarty.

In 1960, Jack Kerouac, chef de file de la "Beat Generation" précisa les rapports de son œuvre avec celle de Proust: "mon œuvre comprend un seul et vaste ouvrage, comme celui de Proust, sauf que mes souvenirs sont écrits à la va vite au lieu de l'être après, dans un lit de malade."[22] Et deux ans plus tard il accorda à Charles Jarvis et à James Curtis un entretien au cours duquel

> il relia sa méthode à celle d'Honoré de Balzac et sa prose à celle de Proust: "J'ai lu *A la recherche du temps perdu*," dit-il, et sur le ton le plus sérieux du monde "et j'ai décidé de faire exactement comme lui— mais vite."[23]

Il faut voir autre chose qu'une simple boutade dans cette déclaration. Jack Kerouac pousse jusqu'à l'absurde la recherche du temps perdu d'une génération en quête d'un passé qui se dérobe et qui ne croit plus à la possibilité de sa récupération par la littérature. L'éthique proustienne a fait son temps.

On peut donc conclure que l'œuvre de Proust a eu une répercussion considérable sur le roman américain entre 1920 et 1960, puisque ses grands représentants, de la Génération perdue à la Beat Generation ont reconnu leur dette vis-à-vis de l'auteur de *la Recherche* non seulement dans leurs commentaires sur son influence mais dans la pratique même de leur écriture.

Il faut distinguer trois grandes phases dans l'accueil que la critique américaine à proprement parler a faite à *A la recherche du temps perdu*. La première va de 1920 à 1932 puisque 1920 marque la date des trois premiers articles consacrés à Proust dans des revues américaines: "The Curious Career of Marcel Proust," anonyme, paraît dans *Current Opinion* de mai, "The Approach to Marcel Proust" par Richard Aldington est publié dans le *Dial* d'octobre et "Marcel Proust" vu par Ellen Fitzgerald occupe trois pages dans *The Nation* de décembre.

Jusqu'à 1932, il y aura une succession de revues de presse en réponse à la publication des différents volumes de l'œuvre de Proust en traduction aux Etats-Unis. Il y aura également quelques articles qui auront pour but d'établir des rapports entre l'homme et l'œuvre. Dans une lettre de juillet 1922 à Gaston Gallimard, Proust se plaint de la façon dont on le présente aux lecteurs américains:

> j'ai été très ennuyé d'un article de M. Pierre de Lanux dans un journal américain, où il raconte que d'abord la *N.R.F.* n'a pas voulu de moi (argent, situation sociale) et ne m'a pris que quand je suis revenu à la charge. Je trouve tout cela sans aucun intérêt et vous me direz alors: "Mais si cela n'a aucun intérêt pourquoi m'en parlez-vous?" Parce que depuis cet article je suis assailli de lettres d'Amérique et de Paris, demandant pourquoi je laisse la *N.R.F.* "se vanter" de m'avoir refusé (chose idiote et d'ailleurs pour moi inintelligible, les rapports de M. de Lanux et de la *N.R.F.* m'étant inconnus, si Antoine Bibesco, qui vient d'arriver à Paris, ne m'avait dit que cet écrivain était votre correspondant en Amérique et avait même écrit à la *N.R.F.* autrefois). En tous cas cet article, où, sachant très mal l'anglais, je n'ai pas compris grand chose, contient beaucoup d'inexactitudes.[24]

Sans doute Marcel Proust eut-il été plus satisfait des pages que lui consacre Joseph Collins en 1923 dans *The Doctor Looks at Literature:* "Marcel Proust Master Psychologist and Pilot of the *vraie vie*" et où il écrit qu' "en novembre 1922 la France a perdu un écrivain dont la renommée égalera celle de Balzac."

En 1925 Edith Wharton publie dans la *Yale Review* un essai enthousiaste qui s'intitule "Marcel Proust," dans lequel elle reconnaît le génie de l'auteur de *la Recherche* mais lui reproche sa peur: "peur de la mort, peur de l'amour, peur de la responsabilité, peur de la maladie, peur des courants d'air, peur de la peur." La même année Edith Rickert fait paraître "Du côté de chez Proust" dans *The New Republic* du 30 septembre;

selon elle, dans *Le Côté de Guermantes* "la méthode analytique a été poussée a un degré jamais rêvé auparavant."

Finalement Proust aura un chapitre de soixante-quinze pages à son nom dans l'ouvrage de Joseph Krutch qui paraît en 1930 sous le titre *Five Masters: A Study in the Mutations of the Novel,* après Boccace, Cervantes, Samuel Richardson et Stendhal. Après avoir donné des éléments biographiques, J. Krutch montre la complexité et l'originalité du roman proustien qui, selon lui, "illustre parfaitement les caractéristiques de ce que Nietzsche appelait l'art Apollonien." Et il conclut qu'il est ridicule de condamner *A la recherche du temps perdu* pour la simple raison que le sujet est en marge des préoccupations des autres romans de l'époque. En un mot ce critique réclame pour l'œuvre de Proust le droit à la différence. Mais c'est l'essai d'Edmund Wilson dans *Axel's Castle: A Study in the Imaginative Literature of 1870-1930,* publié en 1931 par Charles Scribner's Sons à New York, qui va inscrire Proust dans la tradition symboliste et faire ressortir les questions de structure. Selon Edmund Wilson, qui reprend le point de vue de Jacques Rivière, "Marcel Proust est le premier romancier important à appliquer les principes du Symbolisme au roman. . . . Son énorme livre, *A la recherche du temps perdu,* est en fait une structure symphonique plutôt qu'un récit dans le sens commun du terme." Etablissant des parallèles entre la conception du temps chez Proust et les théories d'Einstein, entre la recherche proustienne et l'analyse freudienne, Edmund Wilson pose les bases des grandes directions que prendra par la suite la critique proustienne. En 1931, paraît aussi à New York le *Proust* de Samuel Beckett, première réflexion critique d'un créateur d'univers sur Proust créateur d'univers, œuvre pionnière, qui nous étonne aujourd'hui encore par son extrême modernité.

Dans la *Saturday Review of Literature* du 15 octobre, paraît un tableau des ventes de livres de Proust aux Etats-Unis de la même année (1931) qui s'établit comme suit:

Du côté de chez Swann	39 365 exemplaires
A l'ombre des jeunes filles en fleurs	16 687
Le Côté de Guermantes	4 088
Sodome et Gomorrhe	4 744
La Prisonnière	7 274
Albertine disparue	3 788
Le Temps retrouvé	2 967
	78 913

De 1932 à 1949, on assiste à la montée de la première vague de la critique universitaire américaine parallèlement à l'apparition de centres d'intérêts spécifiques pour un aspect particulier ou un autre d'*A la recherche du temps perdu* et les articles se multiplient dans les revues américaines, au point que Havelock Ellis puisse écrire dans son article sur Marcel Proust dans *Atlantic Monthly* d'octobre 1935: "de nouveaux livres et essais sur Proust sortent des presses en un flot ininterrompu." Lui-même publie chez Houghton Mifflin à Boston un ouvrage critique qui fait date à cause de son titre: *From Rousseau to Proust.* En 1935 donc l'œuvre de Proust est considérée par la critique américaine comme un tournant dans la littérature française. Il serait vain de vouloir ici faire la liste exhaustive de tous les articles parus sur Proust entre 1932 et 1949 mais on peut voir se dessiner de grandes lignes d'approche: Proust comme psychologue est mis à la mode par l'étude de Joseph Warren Beach dans son livre *Twentieth Century Novel* en 1932; les rapports entre la littérature et les autres arts dans *A la recherche du temps perdu* sont étudiés dans des articles divers concernant la musique, la peinture comme "Marcel Proust and Painting" par T. W. Bussom dans la *Romanic Review* de février 1943 ou "The Musical Structure of *Un amour de Swann*" par J. W. Kneller dans la *Yale French Studies* d'avril 1948; dès 1936 on étudie le snobisme et les attitudes sociales de Marcel Proust, ainsi qu'en témoignent divers titres d'articles. On cherche des antécédents à Proust: ainsi Justin O'Brien publie-t-il "La mémoire involontaire avant Proust" dans la *Revue de littérature comparée* de janvier 1939. Et c'est la grande période des comparaisons qui commence avec l'article de David Cabeen, "Saint-Simon et Proust" dans le numéro de juin 1931 des *Publications of the Modern Language Association of America,* et va se poursuivre avec "Bergson's Influence on Marcel Proust" de M. E. Chernowitz dans la *Romanic Review* de janvier 1936 et la comparaison faite par Douglas W. Alden, "Proust and the Flaubert Controversy" dans la même revue mais dans le numéro d'octobre 1937. La même année, David Cabeen propose "A Selected Bibliography of Works on Proust for a Small Library" dans le numéro de décembre de la *French Review* qui constitue la première ébauche d'une bibliographie proustienne systématique, appelée à se développer et à se diversifier au fil des années et dont l'excellence peut se vérifier dans la section Proust de *A Critical Bibliography of French Literature* édité par Douglas W. Alden en 1980. En fait le travail bibliographique de base a été effectué par Douglas Alden aux Etats-Unis, où il a établi sa réputation dès 1940, avec la parution de son remarquable ouvrage: *Proust and His*

French Critics. En 1942, Gladys Dudley Lindner fait le point des réactions de la critique de langue anglaise dans son *Marcel Proust: Reviews and Estimates in English* que publient les Presses de l'Université de Californie.

Très tôt aussi, dès 1931, on s'intéresse à la correspondance de Marcel Proust puisque dans le numéro de juin de *PMLA* paraît un article de Thomas W. Bussom: "Marcel Proust Interpreted Through His Letters." Mais si la bibliographie proustienne est le domaine réservé de Douglas W. Alden, qui fait autorité, la correspondance est celui de Philip Kolb, qui publie en 1948 sa thèse intitulée *La correspondance de Marcel Proust: chronologie et commentaire critique* aux presses de l'Université d'Illinois et qui a préparé depuis diverses éditions des lettres de Proust à sa mère, à Jacques Rivière, etc. . . . et est en train de publier chez Plon l'édition définitive de la correspondance générale de Proust, dont dix-sept volumes sur vingt ont paru à ce jour. Philip Kolb a fait de la bibliothèque de l'université d'Illinois un véritable centre de recherches proustiennes où sont conservés des documents originaux répertoriés par Larkin B. Price dans *A Check List of the Proust Holdings at the University of Illinois* en 1975. Cependant le tout premier article de Philip Kolb touchait à des questions non point de correspondance mais de genèse puisqu'il souligne dans le numéro de mars 1936 de *PMLA* "Inadvertent repetitions of material in *A la recherche du temps perdu.*"

Les problèmes que pose la genèse du roman proustien sont abordés pour la première fois de façon scientifique par un professeur français à Yale, Albert Feuillerat, qui publie en 1934 *Comment Proust a composé son roman.* Ses conclusions seront controversées mais nul ne conteste que son étude est une étape décisive dans la manière de considérer le texte de Proust. Dans la *French Review* de mars 1935, John Spagnoli écrit un article dont le titre explique le contenu: "M. Feuillerat Clarifies Proust." A la même époque, un autre professeur français, Robert Vigneron, qui enseigne à l'université de Chicago, se penche sur les questions de structure de *la Recherche* avec divers articles dans *Modern Philology,* parmi lesquels "Fondements d'une chronologie proustienne" en 1936 et "Structure de Swann" en 1946.

On peut donc dire qu'entre 1932 et 1949 les grands thèmes de la critique proustienne et le traitement des problèmes de méthodologie qu'ils supposent se mettent en place aux Etats-Unis et que le travail critique de base: bibliographie, étude de la correspondance, hypothèses sur la genèse d'*A la recherche du temps perdu,* y fleurit.

Certes il y a des voix dissidentes et des critiques qui n'apprécient pas à sa juste valeur l'envergure de l'entreprise proustienne. Dès 1933, P. E. More écrit à propos d'*Albertine disparue* dans le numéro d'avril de *The American Review* que c'est "le plus bel affichage de futilité larmoyante qu'on ait jamais fait en littérature." Mais dans l'ensemble Proust se vend et se lit selon une courbe ascendante puisque le 26 février 1949, la *Saturday Review of Literature* fait remarquer que "l'œuvre de deux écrivains européens, Franz Kafka et Marcel Proust, dont les carrières respectives touchèrent leur point culminant bientôt après la fin de la première guerre mondiale, passionnent les esprits plus encore aujourd'hui que de leur vivant."

A partir de 1950 et jusqu'à nos jours, les études proustiennes vont s'épanouir dans les universités américaines, où, partout, on enseigne Proust. On assiste à ce que R. Gibson n'hésite pas à appeler "l'avènement des érudits" dans son article sur "Proust et la critique anglo-saxonne." Il faut dire que l'œuvre immense de Proust fournit de multiples sujets de thèse ou de mémoires à des étudiants dont les professeurs commencent à se définir comme spécialistes de Proust vers cette époque. Ainsi, Harold March, qui enseigne la littérature française à Swarthmore College, fait paraître un ouvrage de synthèse *The Two Worlds of Marcel Proust* aux presses de l'Université de Pennsylvanie en 1948. Mais le meilleur exemple est sans doute le professeur Germaine Brée qui publie *Du temps perdu au temps retrouvé: introduction à Marcel Proust* en 1950 (traduit et publié par les presses de Rutgers University en 1955 sous le titre *Marcel Proust and Deliverance from Time*) et forme à l'université de Wisconsin une nouvelle génération de chercheurs proustiens, dont le professeur Theodore Johnson qui fonde en 1969 la *Proust Research Association Newsletter* à l'Université de Kansas. Et en 1951, Germaine Brée définit les nouvelles tendances de la critique proustienne dans le numéro de mai de *Symposium*. En 1963, elle fait le point sur "Les manuscrits de Proust" dans la *French Review* et ouvre de nouvelles perspectives sur l'importance des travaux à faire sur la genèse d'*A la recherche du temps perdu*. Les apports principaux dans ce domaine dont sans doute l'édition critique du *Carnet de 1908* par Philip Kolb dans les *Cahiers Marcel Proust* en 1976 et la publication de l'étude de Douglas W. Alden: *Marcel Proust's Grasset Proofs: Commentary and Variants* aux presses de l'université de Caroline du Nord en 1978.

En 1958, paraît une biographie américaine par Richard H. Barker: *Marcel Proust: A Biography,* publié par Criterion Books à New York. Mais elle sera vite éclipsée, ainsi que tous les autres travaux de ce type d'ailleurs, par la parution en Angleterre du premier tome de la biographie de Proust par George D. Painter, chez Chatto and Windus, en 1959. Immédiatement distribué aux Etats-Unis, le livre y rencontre un grand succès. D'autre part, un premier recueil d'articles critiques est constitué par René Girard, et paraît sous le titre *Proust: A Collection of Critical Essays* en 1962 et plusieurs revues consacrent un numéro spécial à Proust: ainsi *l'Esprit créateur* N° 1 en 1965, puis N° 11 en été 1971, à cause du centenaire de la naissance de Proust, la *Yale French Studies* de juin 1965, et la *Romanic Review* d'avril 1971. En 1974, Larkin B. Price édite *Marcel Proust—A Critical Panorama* (Université d'Illinois) et Barbara Bucknall fait sortir en 1987: *Proust: Essays in Criticism,* chez G. K. Hall à Boston.

On peut voir que l'intérêt porté à l'œuvre de Proust a été constant aux Etats-Unis depuis l'apparition sur le marché américain de *Swann's Way* en 1922 et qu'il a suscité des études en tous genres, ainsi que l'indiquent toutes les bibliographies qui doivent toujours avoir recours à de multiples subdivisions pour couvrir le champs immense des recherches proustiennes qui sont allées en s'élargissant depuis 1950.

Il est vrai que ce sont surtout les milieux universitaires qui ont contribué à consacrer la gloire de Proust en Amérique: jusque-là, tous les étudiants connaissaient au moins *Combray,* grâce à l'édition critique établie par Germaine Brée et Carlos Lynes en 1952. Mais depuis 1980, les choses changent à cause de deux facteurs: la publicité faite en 1981 autour de la nouvelle traduction de *la Recherche* par Terence Kilmartin, que Random House offre en vente promotionnelle à un prix très raisonnable et la parution sur les écrans américains de la version anglaise du film que Volker Schlöndorff a tiré d'*Un amour de Swann* en 1984. Une édition brochée bon marché de *Swann in Love,* avec en couverture Jeremy Irons et Ornella Muti, circule maintenant dans des milieux où le nom de Proust était jusque-là pratiquement inconnu. De nombreux magazines féminins de luxe, comme *Vogue* ou *Vanity Fair* parlent d'une "renaissance proustienne." En un mot, on semble en arriver aujourd'hui, en Amérique, à une popularisation de la lecture de *la Recherche.*

La publication en 1987 de nouvelles éditions critiques du texte de *la Recherche* vient de susciter chez Richard Howard l'idée d'une traduction américaine qui, une fois achevée, devrait permettre aux lecteurs anglophones d'accéder à une version plus fidèle et plus complète de l'œuvre proustienne.

Notes

[1]Gérard Tougas, "Marcel Proust devant la critique anglo-saxonne" in *Revue de Littérature comparée*, n⁰ 30, 1956, p. 103. Cet article donne un bref aperçu des théories avancées par Gérard Tougas dans sa thèse intitulée *Marcel Proust: Aspects of Anglo-American Criticism*, soutenue à l'université de Stanford, Californie, en novembre 1953.

[2]George D. Painter, *Marcel Proust: Les années de maturité*, Paris: Mercure de France, 1966, p. 435.

[3]*Lettres à la N.R.F.* in *Les Cahiers Marcel Proust* 6, Paris: Gallimard, 1934, p. 248.

[4]Bennett Cerf, *At Random: The Reminiscences of Bennett Cerf*, New York: Random House, 1977, p. 99. C'est nous qui traduisons.

[5]Albert Schinz, "Le livre français aux Etats-Unis" in *Revue de Paris*, janvier-février 1936, pp. 893-906.

[6]Cité par Nicholas Joost in *Ernest Hemingway and the Little Magazines*, Barre, Massachusetts: Barre Publishers, 1968, p. 135. C'est nous qui traduisons.

[7]Painter, p. 409.

[8]Cité par James R. Mellow in *Charmed Circle: Gertrude Stein and Company*, New York: Avon Books, 1975, p. 483. C'est nous qui traduisons.

[9]"My great adventure is really Proust. What remains to be written after that?" *The Letters of Virginia Woolf*, éditées par Nigel Nicolson, New York: Harcourt, Brace, 1976, vol. II (1912-22), p. 565.

[10]Francis Scott Fitzgerald, *The Great Gatsby*, New York: Penguin Books, 1926, p. 43.

[11]Marcel Proust, *Du côté de chez Swann*, Paris: Gallimard, 1954, p. 87.

[12]Fitzgerald, p. 117.

[13]Andrew Turnbull, *Scott Fitzgerald: Letters to His Daughter*, New York: Charles Scribner's Sons, 1963.

[14]Loic Bouvard, "Conversation with William Faulkner" in *Modern Fiction Studies*, hiver 1960, pp. 363-64.

[15]Jean Pouillon, *Temps et Roman*, Paris: Gallimard, 1946. Cf. le chapitre "Temps et destinée chez Faulkner," pp. 238-60.

[16]R. P. Adams, "William Faulkner's Apprenticeship" in *Tulane Studies in English*, 1962, p. 138.

[17]*Faulkner at Nogano*, édité par R. A. Jeliffe, Tokyo: Kenkyusha, 1956, p. 44.

[18]*The Letters of Thomas Wolfe*, éditées par Elizabeth Nowell, New York: Charles Scribner's Sons, 1956.

[19]Mary M. Colum, *Literature of Today and Tomorrow*, New York: Charles Scribner's Sons, 1936, p. 102.

[20]*Look Homeward, Angel,* New York: Charles Scribner's Sons, 1929, p. 39. C'est nous qui traduisons.

[21]T. G. Moser, "Thomas Wolfe: Look Homeward, Angel" in *Thomas Wolfe: A Collection of Critical Essays,* édité par Louis D. Rubin, Englewood Cliffs, New Jersey: Prentice Hall, 1973, p. 119.

[22]Seymour Krim, Introduction à *Desolation Angels,* Londres: Panther Books, 1972, p. 19. C'est nous qui traduisons.

[23]"Dialogues in Great Books," Radio Station WCAP, Lowell, Massachusetts, septembre 1963. Cité par E. Jarvis in *Visions of Kerouac: The Life of Jack Kerouac,* Lowell, Massachusetts: Ithaca Press, 1973, p. 178.

[24]*Lettres à la N.R.F.,* p. 220.

4

The Death of Albertine

Nathalie Mauriac Dyer

UNTIL QUITE RECENTLY, the editorial situation of the sequel to *The Captive* was somewhat paradoxical. You could buy the same text under two different titles, "Albertine disparue" or "La Fugitive." And yet neither title actually appeared on any Proustian manuscript. "Albertine disparue" had been given without any understandable reason to the 1925 original edition, completed by the writer's brother Robert. Therefore, the 1954 editors of *Remembrance of Things Past* in the "Bibliothèque de la Pléiade" had preferred to go back to "La Fugitive"—a title at least once intended by Proust, even though abandoned, as his correspondence shows.

In 1986, a typescript corrected by the writer was rediscovered in the effects of Suzy Mante-Proust, Proust's niece. It opens with these words, in the writer's handwriting:

> Ici commence *Albertine disparue,* suite du roman précédent, *La Prisonnière.* (Here begins *Albertine disparue,* sequel to the previous novel, *The Captive.*)

The question of the title seemed at last solved. But there was a *coup de théâtre:* from this typescript of his 1916-17 manuscript, corrected shortly before he died in the fall of 1922, Proust removed three hundred pages, considerably disrupting the continuity of the narrative. He disrupted our reading habits also: although deleted, the three hundred pages were published in the 1925 so-called *Albertine disparue,* and from then on, of course, in all following editions. They belonged for all readers of Proust to the very substance of *Remembrance.* We had thus found a title, only to lose some text. Worse perhaps, to realize that *Remembrance* was even more incomplete than we thought, for Proust would not have made such a crucial emendation without planning some further reorganization of his material. We are led to question how we should now consider *Time Regained*.

It will take some time, no doubt, before the Proustian world admits *Albertine disparue* as it is—a disturbing, disquieting text, confronting editors of *Remembrance of Things Past* with a new and delicate issue, if they want both to respect Proust's last indications and to give a readable, continuous narrative. Simply to go back to the uncorrected version, arguing that Proust could not finish anyway or that he did not *mean* his radical changes, or even that he did not intend *Albertine* for *Remembrance,* is a denial of this issue. If we still want to save the longer version—faithful to it as the narrator to his habits—we should at least give it the abandoned title "La Fugitive." We should not call it "Albertine disparue," for this title would only bring us back to the ambiguous situation I described at the beginning of this talk—without much, if any, justification now.

The rediscovered *Albertine disparue,* published for the first time in 1987, raises many exciting questions for Proustian scholarship. Today I will sketch the death of Albertine, an event that Proust has strikingly redefined, as is suggested by his new title. Let us first recall the circumstances and atmosphere that precede and follow it in the narrative of *Remembrance.* We shall see then how Proust has, in his final version, modified this picture.

Today, October 11, 1988, we should pause to remember Alfred Agostinelli, Proust's chauffeur and secretary. He was born exactly a hundred years ago, October 11, 1888. It is a strange coincidence.

Proust had met him in Cabourg in 1907 and had rehired him in Paris in 1913. But in December of that year Agostinelli had left him quite abruptly and met his death at the end of May 1914. His plane crashed into the Mediterranean. Proust expressed his grief in his correspondence and does not hide his love for him.

The chronology of this drama coincides with changes of importance in the elaboration of *Remembrance of Things Past.* The part played by the girl Albertine develops in new episodes in 1914: her Parisian captivity, her sudden flight, her accidental death and the narrator's following "grief and oblivion." Readers assume that Albertine is, at least partly, Proust's love Agostinelli.

Whether Proust was thinking of Agostinelli when he first wrote of Albertine's fatal accident or not, the death of this character was inevitable in the plot. The real subject of *Remembrance* is "the history of an invisible vocation," the vocation of the narrator. On the slow way to literary achievement, Albertine is one obstacle among many. She embodies the illusions of love, as Venice does those of travelling. She even embodies, briefly, those of art, when she is confused by the narrator in *The Captive* with a work of his. Only her death, followed by her gradual fading from the narrator's memory, will show that she had been from the beginning merely a creature of his imagination—a "ghost" as he says in *Cities of the Plain*.

Necessary to the progress of the whole novel, Albertine's death is foreshadowed from this volume on. First there is an allusion to a grief the narrator will know, comparable to that caused his mother by his grandmother's death. Later Albertine threatens him, saying she will commit suicide by throwing herself into the sea; the narrator points out to her that such a suicide would imitate that of the Lesbian poetess Sappho. Proust links here her threatened suicide to the homosexual theme, which will later be stressed, as we shall see, in her actual death. Further foreshadowings appear when the "narrow black trunks" that she brings as luggage from her stay at Balbec to Paris suggest "coffins" to the narrator; at the end of *The Captive* she will ask Françoise for those trunks before she leaves him.

Shortly before she escapes, Albertine abruptly refuses to give the narrator the kiss that would bring him peace and relief:

> She withdrew with the sort of instinctive and fatal obstinacy of animals that feel the hand of death.

The narrator then adds:

> I know that I then uttered the word death, as though Albertine were about to die. It seems that events are larger than the moment in which they occur, and cannot confine themselves in it. Certainly they overflow into the future through the memory that we retain of them, but they demand a place also in the time that precedes them. One may say that we do not then see them as they are to be, but in memory are they not modified also?

This foreseen death is also a death the narrator obscurely wishes. For he has in the end become the captive of his captive. Albertine is an obstacle, so he thinks, less to his work than to his various fantasies, meeting new girls or travelling to Venice.

This wish will not, however, be expressed directly in *The Captive*. But when the narrator advises Albertine to be very careful on horseback, he seems secretly to hope for an accident that would free him. He will wish it more consciously in *The Fugitive,* but learn at once of the girl's actual death, and be overcome by grief. Proust illustrates here an essential principle of his psychology: the misconstruing of self. The wish for the death of the beloved only shows how little one knows one's own heart. In a parallel demonstration at the end of *The Captive,* immediately after the narrator had told himself he had become quite indifferent to Albertine, he experienced the suffering of her sudden departure.

In the first drafts of *The Captive* and *The Fugitive,* contemporary with the Agostinelli drama of 1914, the wish for Albertine's death was expressed in a much cruder way, in fact as a murder wish:

If she had left me, I would have killed her, for I was in love with her.

When the narrator has learned that Albertine meets girl friends at her aunt's place, where she has lived since her departure, he claims:

If she had not agreed to leave her girl friends, I would have wanted to hit her, to destroy for good in me the suffering I was feeling.

I felt that a mortal blow which would have destroyed her capacity to receive pleasure from others would have removed this suffering from my life.

A following short note indicates that the narrator only now understands some lines from Baudelaire: if we behave with morality, the credit is to be given only to our own cowardice.

These passages will be removed from *The Fugitive* or transferred with noticeable toning down into *The Captive*. A similar one in the sketches of *Time Regained* will also be transformed by Proust into a milder version.

There is of course another major instance of death in *Remembrance,* that of the narrator's grandmother, which has also been given an obvious biographical key. They are quite different and thus complementary experiences for the narrator. While the grandmother's agony is very slow and detailed, the girl's death is instantaneous. Conversely, the mourning over Albertine immediately follows her accident, while the painful realization of the grandmother's irreversible absence takes place long after her actual death, illustrating what Proust calls "the heart's intermissions."

The two events share a major characteristic. They allow the narrator to experience "those strange contradictory impressions of survival and obliteration" inherent in death. Physical disintegration is unable to put an end to the life of the loved one, for she has acquired for the narrator an inner existence, composed of the multiple images of her various appearances at various moments in time:

> For the death of Albertine to be able to suppress my suffering, the shock of the fall would have had to kill her not only in Touraine but in myself. There, never had she been more alive. In order to enter into us, another person must first have assumed the form, have entered into the surrounding of the moment; appearing to us only in a succession of momentary flashes, the person has never been able to furnish us with more than one aspect at a time. (. . .) A great weakness, no doubt, for a person to consist merely in a collection of moments; a great strength also. (. . .) This moment which memory has registered lives still, and with it the person whose form is outlined in it. And moreover this disintegration does not only make the dead person live, it multiplies that person. To find consolation, it was not one, it was innumerable Albertines that I must first forget.

It is because of this life that survives death that the narrator is so eager to learn more about Albertine's actions. Proust writes in *The Fugitive:*

> Since, merely by thinking of her, I brought her back to life, her infidelities could never be those of a dead woman; the moments at which she had been guilty of them became the present moment.

Still jealous of Albertine, but now of her "present" past, the narrator starts various inquiries, sending Aimé to Balbec and then to Touraine. His previous suspicions of the girl's lesbianism are confirmed beyond his worst expectations, through stories obtained from a "doucheuse" ("bathwoman") and a young laundress. Soon he gradually begins to forget Albertine. For

if the life of another consists primarily in the many images we keep of him
or her, his or her real death will occur only when these images have faded in
our memory—in other words, when the loving part in ourself has changed
through time, has in exchange *died*.

This essential process is summed up in one of the sketchbooks of
1914, written during the Agostinelli drama:

> It is not because the others are dead that grief diminishes: it is be-
> cause we ourselves die. Albertine could not have reproached her friend
> with anything, for he has not forgotten her, but joined her in death.

And we read in a contemporary letter of Proust:

> His friend has not forgotten him, poor Alfred. But he joined him in
> death.

Little by little, through the new encounter with Gilberte, "like a
traveller who returns by the same route to his starting point," the narrator
will get closer to the "initial stage of indifference" towards Albertine. It will
be reached during the stay in Venice. A telegram will come, signed with her
name. The earlier telegram, the one from Mme Bontemps, had not killed
Albertine in the heart of the narrator. By a sort of reverse echo, this
telegram, giving the illusion she is still alive, will not succeed in reviving
her. It no longer matters whether she is physically alive or not. Her actual
death for the narrator is complete. In the story Albertine is dead.

It took Proust at least three years, from 1914 to 1916 or 1917, to
finalize the story of *The Captive* and *The Fugitive* in his "Cahiers." In
1921, he writes to his publisher Gallimard that two parts of his novel, "the
death of Albertine, the process of forgetting her," are "the best I have ever
written."

But as the 1922 typescript of *Albertine disparue,* corrected shortly
before he died, shows, Proust has finally modified the death of Albertine
and removed the pages about oblivion. The additions in this last version are
very short. They are yet quite powerful in several ways. In the first version, Albertine had left the narrator to go to her aunt's place in Touraine.

The telegram did not mention more precisely where her accident took place, but the narrator later tells us that it was in this region. In the version of *Albertine disparue,* she meets her death

> au bord de la Vivonne (along the bank of the Vivonne).

The Vivonne is the name Proust gives in *Swann's Way* to the little river that flows near Combray—and Combray is not located in Touraine in the novel.

This mere change of location becomes a unifying stroke that brings together different parts of *Remembrance.* At the moment he reads "the Vivonne" in Mme Bontemps's telegram, the narrator sees Montjouvain in a "flash of lightning." Montjouvain is the name given in *Swann's Way* to another place near Combray, the composer Vinteuil's house. There, many years before, the narrator had caught sight of a scene of love and sadism between Vinteuil's own daughter and a girl friend of hers. Deeply shocked by what he had seen, he had yet forgotten it, until on the little train to Balbec Albertine had mentioned that she was about to join an intimate friend of hers: Mlle Vinteuil's friend herself. Horrified, he had decided to bring her back to Paris at once, and to make her his captive, hoping to prevent her from resuming these relationships. He had enjoyed a temporary relief when in *The Captive* Albertine denied knowing the two lesbians. But the house of Montjouvain is again suggested to him by Mme Bontemps's telegram, and he understands that Albertine left him to join Mlle Vinteuil and her friend.

This turn of events contradicts the previous version. In *The Fugitive,* Albertine proved to be a lesbian too, as Aimé's inquiries showed, but the narrator accepted the idea that she had only an innocent friendship with Mlle Vinteuil's friend.

This major disruption in the story explains why Proust had to remove a large section of the previous version. If he had still wanted the narrator to make inquiries about Albertine's conduct, they ought now to be written from a different perspective, for Albertine's vice was already confirmed in the story.

Proust had prepared the death of Albertine in the first version; he adds to that preparation in the second one. I briefly mentioned that in *The Captive* the narrator advised Albertine to be very careful on horseback:

> I beg of you, my dearest girl, no more of that *haute voltige* you
> were practising the other day. Just think, Albertine, if you were to
> meet with an accident!

On the typescript of this volume, which he was correcting at the
same time as *Albertine disparue,* Proust added:

> Of course I did not wish her any harm. But what a pleasure it
> would be if, with her horses, she should take it into her head to ride off
> somewhere, wherever she chose, and never to return again to my house.
> How it would simplify everything, that she should go and live happily
> somewhere else, I did not even wish to know where!

"I did not even wish to know where!" He will learn it and be
desperate. The last version of Albertine's death illustrates once again the
psychological principle of the misconstruing of self.

To this psychological dimension others are added in the new version. We have just seen its dramatic one; it also has a didactic one. In
Swann's Way, the river Vivonne and the house of Montjouvain are located
on what the narrator calls the two "ways" of Combray: the Vivonne on the
"Guermantes Way" and Montjouvain on the "Méséglise" or "Swann's
Way." These "ways" of Combray seem "diametrically opposed" in space
and symbolize for the narrator two opposite parts of his experience: his discovery of desire and his first artistic impressions. They also give their name
in *Remembrance* to two volumes describing two separate social worlds.

At the news of Albertine's death, the narrator brings together the
Vivonne and Montjouvain, the "Guermantes" and the "Méséglise" ways.
The geographic but also symbolic distances are now abolished; it is the end
of the last beliefs of childhood; perhaps, also, the opening of a new era for
the narrator. Albertine dies on the very "way" where his first artistic
attempts had taken place, as if she wanted to show him what comes after her
death.

The rediscovered version also has a poetic dimension. The last
image of Albertine "along the bank of the Vivonne" evokes the first, when
she was seen by the narrator walking along the seaside at Balbec. Water,
like her, changeable and fugitive, is there, in the background, when she
appears in the story and disappears from it. Titles suggest that this parallel
is no accident: "Albertine disparue" echoes the chapter of *Within a Budding*

Grove called "Albertine apparaît" ("Albertine appears"). Proust died before he could develop it, and we feel the loss of those pages.

Dramatic, didactic, poetic, Albertine's new death also has an effect on the structure of *Remembrance.* By bringing together the two "ways" of Combray, it links *Albertine disparue* to *Swann's Way;* by setting the last image of her beside the first, to *Within a Budding Grove,* and by juxtaposing the Montjouvain on the little train and the one in the telegram, to *Cities of the Plain* and *The Captive.* In his edition of Ruskin's *Sesame and Lilies,* Proust noted that the epigraph was a late addition of the author. It threw light back, said he, on all that was there before. Similarly, the final version of the death of Albertine allows us to see more of the "hidden structure" of *Remembrance of Things Past,* still evolving at the time of Proust's death.

5

De Motu Cordis and *Swann's Way:* Exploring the Circulatory System of Proust's Narrative Technique

Richard M. Ratzan

IN 1628 WILLIAM HARVEY PUBLISHED his *De Motu Cordis,* a landmark in modern medicine celebrated for its description of the circular route of the blood in the human body. Prior to the publication of his book (the title of which means "Concerning the Movement of the Heart"), physicians had various theories about the path of the blood, the most prominent being the Galenic idea that the blood shuttled to and fro between the arterial and venous systems via pores in the ventricular septum of the heart. Harvey set them straight by demonstrating that the blood "has a certain motion as though in a circle."[1]

In this paper I would like to explore the physiology, as it were, of Proust's narrative technique in *Remembrance of Things Past,* using the human circulatory system as a model. There are immediate and evident objections to such an analogy, for example, the nonidentity between a human body and a text and, consequently, the impossibility of a comparison between the two systems. While it might seem true that, unlike the narrative technique of a text, the human circulatory system has only one anatomical structure and thus only one set of biophysiological laws governing the workings of this structure, it is also true that, like a text, the circulatory system admits of different interpretations. For example, the electrical conduction of the heart and its abnormal rhythms are still, despite the vast corpus of information known about them, very much open to exciting and highly theoretical interpretations, as Arthur Winfree demonstrates in his interdisciplinary monograph *When Time Breaks Down.*[2] Too, as Arnold Katz has so ably shown, accepted and apparently secure theories of the biomechanics of the heart have undergone drastic revisions from the 1920s to the present day with profound effects on the therapy of congestive heart failure.[3]

I apologize in advance to medical readers for the simplistic and abbreviated nature of the description of the human circulatory system. Literary readers unfamiliar with the workings of the human body will not find the explanations difficult.

Many authors have commented on the discursive, apparently rambling nature of Proust's narrative technique, called "careless self-indulgent prose" by a prominent American critic as recently as eighteen years ago.[4] Other readers have noted comparisons between the work and other artistic structures, for example, music[5] and the architecture of cathedrals (see below). As Macksey reminds us, Proust himself had the plan of a large structure in mind when he composed *Remembrance of Things Past* and felt that Crémieux's comparison of it to a city was apt.[6] What has not been commonly noted, however, is the comparison between Proust's narrative technique and naturally occurring structures in the physical universe.

Howard Nemerov, in his monograph *The Oak in the Acorn,* approaches this type of comparison when he likens Proust's narrative technique to Hubert Robert's fountain, a fountain that Proust describes in great detail at a party at the Princesse de Guermantes:

> It could be seen from a distance, slender, motionless, rigid, set apart in a clearing surrounded by fine trees, several of which were as old as itself, only the lighter fall of its pale and quivering plume stirring in the breeze. The eighteenth century had refined the elegance of its lines, but, by fixing the style of the jet, seemed to have arrested its life; at this distance one had the impression of art rather than the sensation of water. . . . But from a closer view one realised that, while it respected, like the stones of an ancient palace, the design traced for it beforehand, it was a constantly changing stream of water that, springing upwards and seeking to obey the architect's traditional orders, performed them to the letter only by seeming to infringe them, its thousand separate bursts succeeding only from afar in giving the impression of a single thrust. This was in reality as often interrupted as the scattering of the fall, whereas from a distance it had appeared to me dense, inflexible,

unbroken in its continuity. From a little nearer, one saw that this continuity, apparently complete, was assured, at every point in the ascent of the jet where it must otherwise have been broken, by the entering into line, by the lateral incorporation of a parallel jet which mounted higher than the first and was itself, at a greater altitude which was however already a strain upon its endurance, relieved by a third. From close to, exhausted drops could be seen falling back from the column of water, passing their sisters on the way up, and at times, torn and scattered, caught in an eddy of the night air, disturbed by this unremitting surge, floating awhile before being drowned in the basin. They teased with their hesitations, with their journey in the opposite direction, and blurred with their soft vapour the vertical tension of the shaft that bore aloft an oblong cloud composed of countless tiny drops. . . .[7]

Although the fountain can be a work of nature's art, e.g., a geyser, Robert's fountain—and therefore Proust's metaphor—are still objects in the world of man-made art. Nemerov noted, briefly, the similarity between this metaphor and Proust's "radical, exfoliating method, which is as it were that of a tree that branches as it grows."[8] I would like to develop the similarity between Proust's narrative technique and another system in the natural world, the human circulatory system. An analysis of the underlying relationship between their respective structures and the function they have in common, that is, maximizing the flow of information in a given space with time, will lead to implications for Proust's text that accompany such an interpretation.

One can see in many structures in the physical world the same fanlike organization of materials seen in a fountain. A few examples are lightning (see the cover of the November 1988 *Scientific American*), a snowflake, many types of coral, and fractals, a new field of mathematics that explores the boundary between order and disorder—the minute exploding surfaces of naturally occurring edges. Incidentally, this fanning is also seen in the arch, especially the cathedral arch, which figures so prominently in the architecture of *Remembrance of Things Past,* as several critics, including Macksey and, most recently, J. T. Johnson, Jr., have noted.[9] Indeed, in an unpublished letter Proust admits that he had, at one time, wanted to name sections of the book after the parts of a cathedral.[10]

A fanlike structure is also encountered in the human body, where it increases the surface area of detail. In so doing, it is "solving" this same space-filling challenge, i.e., it is providing the maximum information per unit of stable volume. This form is the basis for the shape of a snowflake, a tree, a Turkish towel, the microstructure of a computer chip, and a long queue awaiting a double-decker bus in London. A convoluted, branching, redundant line is the most effective way to pack the most information, i.e., orderly (or stable) material, into a given space. The key words here are "information" and "space." It is easier, in many systems, to get more disorderly material, or "noise" (as opposed to information), into a given space. Consider the microchip. One could probably fit more millimeters of circuitry onto the chip if they were packed into every cubic nanometer leaving no gaps anywhere. The gain in material would be the loss in order.

To appreciate the human circulatory system as a biological analogue of Proust's narrative technique, it will be helpful to begin with the heart and proceed to the blood vessels, the highways and byways of the circulation, moving, as we do, from macro- to microstructural levels of branching and complexity. The conducting system, or "wiring" of the heart, conducts electrical activity throughout the heart in a highly orderly fashion, beginning at the sino-atrial (SA) node, the center of the center of the body as it were. (See Figure 1, opposite.)

The cells in the SA node are called "pacemaker cells" since they automatically fire, rest, and then refire, setting the pace of the heart beat for the other cells in the heart. In other words, unlike most cells in the body, they need no stimulus to fire. As such they are but one of several types of automatically firing cells in the heart. They happen to be the fastest to fire after resting. Thus, they fire before any of the other automatically firing cells in the heart have a chance to "go off." As the electrical message spreads throughout the heart in a radial manner, millions of muscle fibers contract synchronously. It is especially important to note that the route of activation begins its journey over a roughly symmetrical pair of "bundles." There is, therefore, a precisely linked spatial and temporal sequence of the dissemination of electrical activity (information), leading to a coordinated series of rhythms. This series of rhythms takes the form of regularly recurring pulses of electrical and muscular activity that we recognize as the heart beat and pulse, respectively. This spatial and temporal dichotomy will play a prominent role in the comparison between the human circulatory system and Proust's narrative technique.

After it leaves the heart via the aorta, some of the arterial blood first enters the coronary vessels, those blood vessels that branch off the aorta to

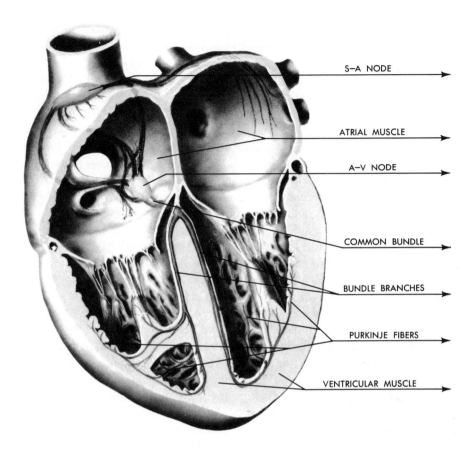

S–A NODE

ATRIAL MUSCLE

A–V NODE

COMMON BUNDLE

BUNDLE BRANCHES

PURKINJE FIBERS

VENTRICULAR MUSCLE

©CIBA

Figure 1

supply the heart itself. There is a gradual and uniform diminution of vessel size as each coronary blood vessel gets farther and farther away from the aorta. In other words, as the blood vessel supplies increasingly smaller areas of the body, in this instance heart muscle, the caliber of the blood vessel continually decreases. This tapering is as true for the blood vessels in the body as it is for Proust's narrative technique, as I shall demonstrate below.

The aorta delivers arterial blood to the whole body. This arterial circulation (also called the "left" circulation) supplies the billions of cells in the body with nutrients in the form of food and oxygen. The venous (or "right") circulation completes the loop, returning from the cells to the heart, picking up waste and then becoming reoxygenated in the lungs prior to its recirculation as arterial blood.

Of interest in considering the macrocirculation, that is, the circulation of the body as a whole, is the presence of these paired circuits (left and right circulations) that at first glance seem to have nothing to do with one another. They are, however, structurally and mechanically quite similar and go to (as the left circulation) or return from (as the right circulation) all the same places. There are significant differences, however. For example, the arterial circulation has a muscular layer that helps propel the arterial blood forward. The venous side has valves to prevent the blood from falling backward between beats of the heart. There are still other differences that make these circulations symmetrical but not mirror images, for example, their different responses to nervous, hormonal, and mechanical stimuli.

Important to our analogy is the existence, between these two circulations, of a connection that corresponds in a microscopic way to the macroscopic connection between the arterial and venous circulations. Although the caliber of the arteries and arterioles gradually decreases, it symmetrically and just as gradually increases on the venous side. What is between these two circulations is the microcirculation of the capillary system, a microscopic lacework of vessels that takes the blood to, and then from, the individual cells of the body. A tissue network of vessels often the thickness of one or two red blood cells, the capillary system is a series of transitional vessels connecting the arterial and venous sides. The arterial blood must traverse this series of tissue bridges to regain access to the venous circulation. (See Figure 2, opposite.)

HOW exactly is *Swann's Way* like the heart or the human circulatory system? As I shall demonstrate, the textual correspondences are many

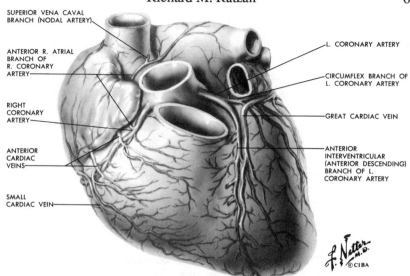

SUPERIOR VENA CAVAL
BRANCH (NODAL ARTERY)

ANTERIOR R. ATRIAL
BRANCH OF
R. CORONARY
ARTERY

RIGHT
CORONARY
ARTERY

ANTERIOR
CARDIAC
VEINS

SMALL
CARDIAC VEIN

L. CORONARY ARTERY

CIRCUMFLEX BRANCH OF
L. CORONARY ARTERY

GREAT CARDIAC VEIN

ANTERIOR
INTERVENTRICULAR
(ANTERIOR DESCENDING)
BRANCH OF L.
CORONARY ARTERY

Figure 2

and varied but strikingly in line with the structural and physiological details of the human circulatory system. Since *Swann's Way* is the occasion of this celebration, I have emphasized, wherever possible, this text.

The first and most obvious point of comparison is the central role—a controlling role to be sure—of the narrator, who is the heart of the novel. *Swann's Way* starts *in medias res,* that is, it originates from the center of the center of the novel: it begins at the (artistically) central time of the narrative center, Marcel. All characters and memories follow what Richard Macksey calls the "flight from the center of the self."[11] Moss agrees: "The structure of his book cannot by intention be chronological. It is, rather, centrifugal."[12] Like the human circulatory system, the narrative action is circular: it emanates from Marcel, embraces all characters, and, in a manner described below, eventually returns to Marcel for recirculation, this time reoxygenated as art.

On a more structural level, there is a macroscopic fanlike structure similar to both the text and the human circulatory system. For example, if one begins to outline the Overture section of *Swann's Way* in a conventional, hierarchical fashion, one obtains the following:

SWANN'S WAY
Overture

     3-11 sleep-waking
       3-5 child
       5-6 dream of adult women
       6-8 personal existence questioned
       8-11 spatial confusion—child's and adult's
    11 awake: memory
    11-60 Combray: childhood—magic lantern
        14-16 grandmother's walks
         17-18 dreaded goodbye from mother
      18-60 Swann's visits
        18-32 Swann's visits in general
         18-20 M. Swann elder
          20-29 Swann's real vs perceived image
          26-27 Mme de Villeparisis knows Swann
          28-29 Duc de X knows Swann
          29-30 Swann gives Asti; Swann in *Figaro*
          31 Narrator's foreboding of a visit by Swann
          32-48 real Swann visit
            32-33 Swann arrives
            34-36 Aunts "thank" Swann for Asti
            37-40 narrator and Françoise
          41-42 narrator waits for mother—thwarted love
            42-44 Swann's love for Odette equally thwarted
            45-46 narrator waits for mother; Swann leaves
          46-48 family discusses Swann
          48-49 narrator greets mother
          49-50 father permits reunion
          51-60 mother and narrator in bedroom
            51 narrator reminisces back and forward
            52 narrator's affection a nervous condition
          53 sadness
          54-59 mother reads
            54-57 various works = grandmother's taste
            55-57 merit of antique time
          57-59 *François le Champi:*
          59 agony soothed
          60-66 "And so": lying awake at Combray: memories
          60-61 Combray and past—DEAD
        61-66 Madeleine
     67-3000+ *RTP*

If, however, one outlines this subtext nonhierarchically (an exercise that is valid for much of Proust, whose text can be called the first large textual nonhierarchical data base), one sees the following morphology:

SWANN'S WAY
Overture

3-5 child
5-6 dream of adult women
6-8 personal existence questioned
8-11 spatial confusion—child's and adult's
11 awake: memory
14-16 grandmother's walks
17-18 dreaded goodbye from mother
18-20 M. Swann elder
20-29 Swann's real vs perceived image
26-27 Mme de Villeparisis knows Swann
28-29 Duc de X knows Swann
29-30 Swann gives Asti; Swann in *Figaro*
31 Narrator's foreboding of a visit by Swann
32-33 Swann arrives
34-36 Aunts "thank" Swann for Asti
37-40 narrator and Françoise
41-42 narrator waits for mother—thwarted love
42-44 Swann's love for Odette equally thwarted
45-46 narrator waits for mother; Swann leaves
46-48 family discusses Swann
48-49 narrator greets mother
49-50 father permits reunion
51 narrator reminisces back and forward
52 narrator's affection a nervous condition
53 sadness
54-57 mother reads
55-57 merit of antique time
57-59 *François le Champi:* fine rhythmic utterances
59 agony soothed
60-61 Combray and past—DEAD
61-66 Madeleine
67-3000+ *RTP*

Note there is still a main stalk, or trunk, with branching nodes. And there is still a forward movement that is all but obscured by the wealth of apparently tangential, unrelated details. But the relationship is not clearly or classically hierarchical with subordinate relationships or interrelationships. Rank-ordering the different digressions in any *hierarchical* manner, when the digressions have no clear relationship to each other, is arbitrary. Rather, like the "spirit of the times, following its habitual course which advances by digression, inclining first in one direction, then in the other,"[13] Proust's narrative technique, despite many tangents, "always moves on. The *Search* remains fundamentally a story—a temporal linear narrative."[14] When we consider the original handwritten mss and their dendritic *inédits,* tangential buds of text, and interminable marginal scions, the analogy is all the more striking.

Advancing to the microscopic level of Proust's text, that is, the microcirculation of the sentence, we see a structure that recreates, like the human circulatory system, its own macrostructure. As Thibaudet wrote,

> This mode of picturing a world implies a world in the way the sentence is put together,—that synthesizing kind of sentence which seems indefinitely extensible and which holds in germ already, as in a homoeomery of Anaxagoras, all the complexity of the book, just as the book offers for our grasp all the complexity of life.[15]

Parsing the fountain passage quoted above, we observe the following (See parsed sentence in Figure 3, opposite): It doesn't require too much imagination, after one has rotated this parsed sentence ninety degrees counterclockwise, to see that the description of this fountain (of water) is itself a fountain (of words). The microstructure informs the macrostructure. Or, as Thibaudet would put it, the "germ" of the fountain is in the sentence depicting the fountain. In describing the fountain, the words are describing themselves and their method.

This "radical, exfoliating method," to recall Nemerov's description of it, informs the narrative technique of Proust at all levels of organization and complexity. As Shattuck observes, in a Proustian sentence "subordination serves to arrange a large amount of material around the clause."[16] This is a prose stylist's way of solving the space-filling problem facing any informational system. *Remembrance of Things Past* is but a microchip of words writ large.

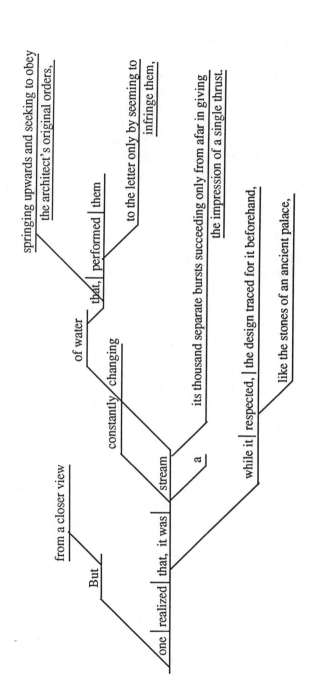

Figure 3

Looking at the cellular level of the text, that is, considering the characters and thematic subjects as cells, we see incredibly intricate interactions between Swann and Odette, Charlus and narrator, Charlus and Jupien, Charlus and Morel, etc.—all interacting at microsurfaces rich in details. This attention to the minute truths of life constitutes what Rivière terms the nibbling technique of Proust, calling him a "rodent."[17] Ortega y Gasset is said to have called Proust a "near-sighted genius."[18] Proust himself calls his work a kind of microscope or magnifying glass.[19] However, as the latter passage illustrates (*RTP* [Kilm] III: 1098-99), Proust's sights are ever on distant truths and "laws, great distances and major generalities."[20] Moss also notes this oscillation between the microscope and telescope, likening it to a zoom lens and making the important observation that Proust preserves the integrity of this optical metaphor by maintaining the proportion ("ratio to distance") between microscopic and macroscopic.[21] This observation is as true for snowflakes and fractals as it is for blood vessels and is but an optical equivalent to Thibaudet's "germ" analogy.

Certain thematic and conceptual phenomena seem to fit this comparison of Proust's narrative technique to the human circulatory system as well. The first is the presence of rhythms, or resonances. Indeed, Georges Poulet calls the entire novel "one immense 'resonance box.' " Shattuck calls them narrative refrains. For Deleuze they are a kind of "autorepetition . . . [that] . . . re-unites different objects."[22]

Some examples of the narrative rhythms that circulate through the text, recycling the same information in forms that differ only slightly from their preceding and subsequent forms, follow:

There is the rhythm of Swann and the narrator as paired dualities. Their attitudes to the same character, for example, Bergotte, or corresponding characters, for example, Odette and Albertine, are continually compared and contrapuntally contrasted. Their views on art, the Guermantes family, the Vinteuil sonata, the Dreyfus affair—all are carefully evoked to suggest parallels between the two. Macksey notes a homologous parallel between Charlus and Swann.[23] Each time one or the other explicates his view on a subject present in the other's experience as well, a rhythm is established or, if already established, reinforced.

Another rhythm is the cadence of self-analysis that constantly recurs throughout the text, rhythmically, like the circulation. It pulsates throughout thousands of pages performing the same function as the heart beat, that is, keeping the solid fountain of self-analysis dynamically intact.

A third rhythm is the theme of parallel selves, the self as same but somehow now different. A character will perceive himself as changed and compare himself with his former self. Or the narrator will make this comparison. Swann furnishes many instances of such evolutionary changes of self (some gradual but many, as here, defined by punctuated epiphanies of insight). He becomes himself again but now in thraldom to Odette[24] and becomes a new being after Odette's acceptance of an invitation from him. Swann recognizes himself, during the playing of the Vinteuil Sonata, as a wretched figure, an insight that fills him with such pity that he cries.[25] The narrator observes in Swann a duality that represents the faintness of his love for Odette and his desire to remain her lover.[26] Again, Swann sees himself as two characters, a young man and his present self.[27]

Similarly, as noted above with respect to the rhythms of identification of Swann with Marcel, the latter also experiences a doubling as a result of love. A few pages after Marcel sees the Gilberte Swann of the present and the girl of his youth as "two different people,"[28] Marcel sees himself and Gilberte as an almost vertiginous pairing of doubles:

> They (these new pleasures) were given, not by the little girl whom I loved to the "me" who loved her, but by the other, the one with whom I used to play, to that other "me" who possessed neither the memory of the true Gilberte, nor the inalienably committed heart which alone could have known the value of a happiness which it alone had desired.[29]

In *The Fugitive* Marcel observes that, in no longer loving Albertine, " 'the man that I was, the fair-haired young man, no longer exists, I am another person.' "[30] This in turn reinforces the rhythm of the Swann-Marcel identification, recalling Swann's realization, while giving instructions to the barber, that he is no longer in love with Odette.[31]

Many other narrative refrains exist, for example, the metaphor of the malady of love; the jealous possessor (Swann, Marcel) possessing not a lover (Odette, Albertine) but nothing; the numerous biblical allusions; and the identification of characters with works of art. Each time any recurs, a new pulse adds its individual jet to the stream of the whole.

Another conceptual comparison between the human circulatory system and Proust's narrative technique is symmetry. It is equally true for both that they are NOT mirror-images. We use this fact all the time in medicine, particularly in orthopedics and neurology, for example, in examining a patient for the neurologic symptoms of hysteria. This symmetry that is pairing but not exact, a phenomenon that Deleuze terms "difference and repetition" and which Brée identifies as reverberations that are never exactly duplicated (recall the rhythm of parallel selves, above), raises another correspondence between Proust's narrative technique and the human circulatory system, i.e., the "two ways" in *Remembrance of Things Past*.[32] Swann's way and the Guermantes way are a controlling metaphor for a host of associated secondary metaphors, such as the aristocracy and bourgeoisie, love and art, etc.

Swann's way, named for its passage along the boundary of Swann's estate, was also known as the Méséglise way, after the village of Méséglise-la-Vineuse, its terminus. This walk began at the front door in Combray, a door that opened on the Rue du Saint-Esprit. Shorter than the Guermantes way, Swann's way traversed a plain and offered the wind as a companion for Marcel, who first sees the variety of sex while on this path— the indecent gesture of Gilberte and the homosexual sadistic love between Vinteuil's daughter and her lover.

The Guermantes way, an eponymous route named for the landed and wealthy Guermantes family, started through the little garden gate that dropped the walkers into the Rue des Perchamps, dotted with grass plots over which two or three wasps would spend the day botanizing (with proleptic resonances, that is, rhythms, of Charlus and Jupien). The Guermantes way is a longer, scenic route by the riverside of the Vivonne. It is here that Marcel decides to become an artist, first feels self-doubt about this goal, and observes the value of perspective while looking at the three steeples of Martinville and Vieuxvicq and their changing relationships as he travels along this route.[33]

Thus Swann's way and the Guermantes way are paired but not mirror images, two ways that have a biological symmetry: they start from different doors of the house in Combray, are taken for different purposes (never on the same day), with different memories along their routes and come to stand for apparently radically different events, concepts, and persons. Swann's way "stands for" art, love, bourgeoisie; the Guermantes way, for aristocracy and society. Swann's way and the Guermantes way were separate and without geographical or ideological communication (at least in the book *Swann's Way*). As the narrator says, "I set between them, far more than the mere distance in miles that separated one from the other, the distance that there was between the two parts of my brain in which I used to think of them, one of those distances of the mind which not only keep things apart, but cut them off from one another and put them on different planes."[34]

The two ways *do* eventually connect, of course, as we all know. And they connect via transversals, or connections, as Deleuze astutely elaborates.[35] Some of these transversals are as follows: Marcel never "penetrates" the village of Méséglise-la-Vineuse (of the Méséglise way) or the source of the Vivonne (the river of the Guermantes way). Gilberte Swann (of Swann's way) becomes the wife of Saint-Loup (of the Guermantes way). Odette (of Swann's way) later becomes the lover of the Duc de Guermantes, and Mme de Verdurin becomes the Princesse de Guermantes! The Vinteuil sonata freely communicates between the two with respect to its composition (in Swann's way) and its performance (at parties in both worlds, for example, chez Verdurin and Guermantes). Deleuze writes that transversality "constitutes the singular unity and totality of the two ways without suppressing their difference or distance." Shattuck writes that they "represent most basically the action of metaphor itself— different elements folding into one."[36]

One can now easily appreciate how the two ways resemble the human circulatory system in their representing symmetrical but not identical "circulations" and in their uniting via a system of transversals analogous to the capillary circulation. (See Figure 4, following page.) The two ways of Proust's text, like the two circulations, are two routes in parallel that develop in series. They both progress to their ultimate development at a most basic level, at which point in time and space they join. In their circularity and union their separate identities become, while not indistinguishable, less different than alike. Their similarities multiply; their differences add.

If this analogy between Proust's narrative technique and the human circulatory system is a successful one it is so because *Remembrance of Things Past* can be described as an organic text. That is, it "behaves" in much the same way an organism behaves. As Germaine Brée observes, "Composition and style are simply the means whereby Proust constructs a novel organically bound to the general vision from which it originated."[37] In ways that I shall explore below, the composition (anatomy) and style (physiology) of *Remembrance of Things Past* share many characteristics with living organisms. Taking the human circulatory system as but one system in the organism called man was one way to demonstrate this broader analogy. I could have just as easily and validly used the endocrine system

Vein   Capillaries   Artery
              (Microcirculation)

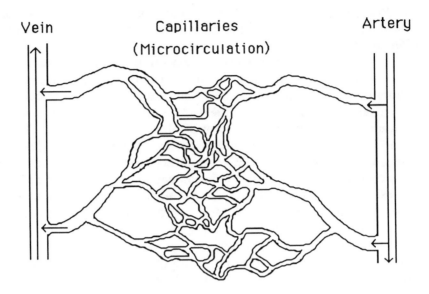

Figure 4

or the nervous system or the musculoskeletal system. Each would have illustrated, insofar as each follows the same biomechanical principles followed by other systems in the body, the similarities between these operating principles and Proust's narrative technique. Each would have highlighted different aspects of Proust's narrative technique that resemble that system's peculiar constraints and properties. For example, in comparing Proust's narrative technique to the endocrine system, we see immediately the similarities between key words as syntactic hormones and characters as receptors, e.g., botanizing, bees, Jupien, Charlus, and homosexuality.

The view of *Remembrance of Things Past* as an organic text has some interesting consequences, consequences that such a comparison invites and, if the comparison is to stand, demands. The first is that such a metaphor would predict that the most significant interactions are at the cellular, minute level. It is here that further research is needed, for example, the study of interrelationships between characters like Swann and Odette.

Thus the study of Swann and Odette as Swann and Odette in love moves up a level of complexity. Yet we need to examine, as in the body, an even finer level of order and disorder moving to the very fringe of organization and function, for example, Swann and Odette as an example of jealous love or, even more microscopically, Swann and Odette when the jealousy is homosexually directed. Then and only then will we reap maximum benefit by comparing the discoveries at this microscopic level of study with the comparably microscopic level of study when the subjects are Marcel and Albertine in their homosexually directed jealousy. It is this study of one theme serially, or the juxtaposition of parallel series (compare Deleuze's discussion of each love assuming a "serial form"[38]) of loves that yields the finest rewards. Such study is, arguably, only possible in an organic text as rich as Proust's where the "germ" of one level, to repeat Thibaudet's term, is present in a lower level. The same can be said of manipulation of one character by another, whether it is Morel and Charlus or Jupien and Charlus or Saint-Loup and Marcel.

In addition to the study of characters at their cellular level, we would do well to study semantic and syntactical units at their most microscopic functioning, for example, the repetitive use of words like "penetrate" and "chrysalis" and phrases like sealed vessels ("vases clos").[39] As Richard Howard has noted, "language binds this book together in other ways than simple linear structure."[40] One such way is the presence of micro-rhythms of vocabulary, grammar, and syntax that reverberate throughout the text, setting up, in turn, other micro-rhythms and contributing to larger structures and rhythms.

Yet another consequence of this analogy is the phenomenon, in both organic texts and living organisms, wherein chance combines with the "normal" routine of life to produce unexpected conditions. Some of these conditions are felicitously desirable; others are pathologic, perhaps even disruptive to the organism. For example, in the heart of some otherwise normal people are accessory conducting pathways that circumvent the usual paths from the sino-atrial node to the conducting system in the ventricle. Impulses rarely go down this accessory shortcut, but when they do they can set up a cyclical, repetitive rhythm in the heart that is usually benign. Disturbing to the person but usually self-limiting. (Occasionally, the rhythm is not self-limiting and not benign.)

Analogous to this fortuitous combination of normal and abnormal rhythms is the phenomenon of involuntary memory in *Remembrance of Things Past*. The memories elicited by a madeleine or uneven cobblestones represent a textual parallel. It is a fortuitous event that triggers an

independent process that is as free from the subject's control in the story as
a repetitive heart beat is in any patient.

In both systems an "abnormal" confluence of new circumstances,
that is, spatial and temporal circumstances in the present, and old circumstances, that is, spatial and temporal circumstances in the past, leads to
unexpected conditions of excitation. The stimuli in the text, like those in the
body, are unique, not manipulable (in terms of intentionally reproducing the
excitatory milieu) or easily controlled once started. They both produce
events (heart beats, memories) that are qualitatively similar each time but
unique in specifics. All eighteen examples of involuntary memory in
Remembrance of Things Past are different and unleash different
memories.[41] Poulet calls the act of remembering synthetic, not analytical.
Likewise, Shattuck calls such excited moments "composite states."[42]

On a more conceptual level, the same process occurs between reader
and text. The same confluence of events, text, specific experiences and
memories that any individual reader brings to each text unavoidably leads to
sudden explosions of personal meaning, flashes of idiosyncratic understanding. Proust facilitates such confluences insofar as the textual rhythms
we have discussed connect virtually any single part of the text with another.
This interconnectedness increases the chance that a reader will suddenly
experience such an echo of significance that involves that subtext, another
connected subtext, and the reader. Germaine Brée locates this interconnectedness in Proust's use of the word "comme":

> By the abundant use he makes of it, Proust is able to evoke around and
> inside his world all possible ramifications [note the inescapable use of a
> branching, radiating metaphor] without ever committing his novel to
> any one; its integrity is intact. Everything in his world is interrelated
> and reverberates from the realm of sensitivity to the intellectual,
> emotional, or moral realm, but the correspondences are never really
> "defined."[43]

This interrelatedness becomes an amalgam of the reader's memory of these
texts in previous readings and the reader's memory of events in his own life
that connect experientially with these past and present texts.

Yet another reasonable expectation of an organic text is the
biological marking of time, that is, time measured by change, increments or
decrements or ratios, not by absolute numbers. Certainly this is true of

Remembrance of Things Past, a text in which there is never any anchoring in time by numbers—only by current events, like the Dreyfus affair, the appearance of automobiles, etc. Time, like the thermometers in *The Magic Mountain,* is measured but not calibrated. True biological time is relative to itself and to the physical world, a close but never precise exactitude. For example, the heart beat, even when apparently fast and regular during exercise, varies from, say, 144 to 145 per minute. It is *not* an atomic clock. It is *not* a computerized machine. In fact, as a recent report emphasizes, it is only when the heart becomes unhealthy that it becomes regular, signaling, in some critically ill persons, impending death.[44]

In both types of organisms we would predict the components to undergo eventual degeneration and death. There should be a running down of the biological clock, a coming to an end, a decaying, what Revel calls "decomposition."[45] And yet, like a fountain, or an Heraclitean stream, we never see the change except with sudden static insights. These insights are mental photographs, magic lantern slides of a slice of time, a fragment of a life. In both the human organism and the text-as-organism we see the changes statically and never dynamically. In medicine we take x-rays, biopsies of organs (which are Proust's "slices" of time). In *Remembrance of Things Past* we have Swann's sudden realization that he is a wretched man in love (crying at this insight) or the frieze of old, withered faces in the final soirée.

Lastly, we would expect to see in both the human circulatory system and Proust's narrative technique an attempt to reproduce the organism. And in both we do. At the end of *Remembrance of Things Past* we see Marcel, who is different from all other characters in that *he* is the writer, become the pacemaker cell—the initiator of all the other coordinated rhythms.[46] *He* automatically begins the story, that is, the rhythm, again at the end of each cycle. And each time *we* read the text we cannot do so without the ending giving birth, automatically, to the beginning. *Remembrance of Things Past* is a regenerative text. Shattuck utilizes loops and figure-of-eights to illustrate the regenerative nature of *Remembrance of Things Past,* diagrams that bear no slight resemblance to the macrocirculation of the human circulatory system.[47]

The implications of such a regenerative text are interesting, especially for a text continually investigating the workings of memory. We have a human organism with unique and changing neural rhythms reading a text-as-organism with unique, biologically similar rhythms. Since both organisms change with each reading, Beckett is correct in asserting that "the observer infects the observer with his own mobility" leading to "two separate and immanent dynamisms related by no system of synchronisation."[48] Thus the uniqueness of each time that the reader reads *Remembrance of Things Past* in a particular spot at a particular time means a unique memory of text. As Nemerov writes, "the novel has become its own memory."[49]

Remembrance of Things Past is quintessentially a book about time and change and how humans invest these two ineluctable phenomena with meaning within their own lives. Proust realized that the most effective mode of translating the paradoxical notion of change within permanence was to use static images that he then develops and analyzes over a long time. Hence Proust's fascination with optics, magic lantern images, slices, fragments, painted, written, sculpted and dramatic artistic works—all opposed to the parade of an individual personality through life, the continuum of music, the cinema of memory. This contrast of dynamic and static, pulsating with flowing, branching with streaming, is at the heart of the fountain metaphor of Robert's structure and Proust's narrative technique. It is at once the basis for a favorite phrase in the novel and even the intended title for Proust's entire work.

When Swann's father said that he used to think of his dead wife often but never much at any one time, the phrase " 'Often, but a little at a time, like poor old Swann' " became one of the favorite sayings of Marcel's grandfather.[50] Perhaps this is what Proust had in mind when he wrote his publisher, Gaston Gallimard, on April 6, 1912, proposing *Les Intermittences du Cœur* as the general title for his masterpiece.[51] Certainly M. Swann the elder was suffering emotional intermittences of the heart in his grief, just as the metaphor of an intermittent heart beat needed to maintain a constant flow of life is the biological equivalent of Robert's fountain and the artistic equivalent of Proust's narrative technique. Early in his own masterpiece, Harvey wrote that by dissecting live animals one could observe that "the heart sometimes moves, sometimes rests, and that there is a time in which it moves and a time in which it stops moving."[52] The authors of *Intermittences of the Heart* and *De Motu Cordis* understood the inherently pulsatile and circular nature of the objects of their study equally well, were geniuses in their materials and methods, and left us revolutionary triumphs describing their research.

I would like to thank Arnold M. Katz, M.D., Professor of Medicine and Head, Division of Cardiology, the University of Connecticut School of Medicine, for continued support and inspiration during the writing of this essay.

Notes

All references to the English edition of *Remembrance of Things Past* will be to Marcel Proust, *Remembrance of Things Past,* trans. C. K. Scott Moncrieff and Terence Kilmartin, New York: Random House, 1981, and will be noted as *"RTP* (Kilm) vol. no: page no."

[1] William Harvey, *Exercitatio Anatomica de Motu Cordis et Sanguinis in Animalibus,* Francofurti, 1618: 41 (author's translation).

[2] Arthur Winfree, *When Time Breaks Down,* Princeton: Princeton University Press, 1987.

[3] Arnold M. Katz, "Molecular Biology in Cardiology, a Paradigmatic Shift," *Journal of Molecular Cell Cardiology* 20 (1988): 355-66.

[4] William Gass, *New York Times Book Review,* vol. 120, sect. 7, July 11, 1971: 1, 2, 12, 15.

[5] Joseph Wood Krutch, Introduction, in Marcel Proust, *Remembrance of Things Past,* trans. C. K. Scott Moncrieff, vol. 1, New York: Random House, 1934: xi ff; André Maurois, "Marcel Proust," *From Proust to Camus,* New York: Doubleday, 1968: 17; Milton Hindus, *Proustian Vision,* Carbondale, Illinois: Southern Illinois University Press, 1954: 40 ff.

[6] Richard Macksey, "Architecture of Time: Dialectics and Structure." *Proust: A Collection of Critical Essays,* ed. René Girard, Englewood Cliffs, NJ: Prentice-Hall, Inc., 1962: 104-05.

[7] *RTP* (Kilm), II: 680-81.

[8] Howard H. Nemerov, *The Oak in the Acorn: On "Remembrance of Things Past" and on Teaching Proust, Who Will Never Learn,* Baton Rouge: Louisiana State University Press, 1987: 115.

[9] Macksey, 105-07; J. T. Johnson, Jr., "Marcel Proust and Architecture: Some Thoughts on the Cathedral-Novel," *Critical Essays on Marcel Proust,* ed. Barbara J. Bucknall, Boston: G. K. Hall, 1987: 133-61.

[10] Macksey, 105.

[11] Macksey, 105.

[12] Howard Moss, *The Magic Lantern,* New York: Macmillan, 1962: 18.

[13]*RTP* (Kilm), II: 845.

[14]Roger Shattuck, *Marcel Proust,* New York: Viking, 1974: 110.

[15]Albert Thibaudet, "Faces of Proust," *Proust: A Collection of Critical Essays,* ed. René Girard, op. cit.: 50. Shattuck describes a Proustian sentence as one that moves "through long spirals" (*Marcel Proust:* 28), which in turn suggests the correspondence between Proust's narrative technique and the analogous informational helix of the human body's "germ," that is, DNA. In describing the sentence, "But whereas. . ." (*ROTP* [Kilm] I: 213), Shattuck seems to be paraphrasing Thibaudet almost exactly when he writes that this sentence "contrives . . . to suggest the whole sinuous course of their love affair" (*Marcel Proust:* 30).

[16]Shattuck, 30.

[17]Jacques Rivière, "Analytic Tradition," *Proust: A Collection of Critical Essays,* ed. René Girard, op. cit.: 43.

[18]Henri Peyre, "The Legacy of Proust," *Proust: A Collection of Critical Essays,* ed. René Girard, op. cit.: 41.

[19]*RTP* (Kilm) III: 1089, 1098-99.

[20]Gilles Deleuze, *Proust and Signs,* trans. Richard Howard, New York: G. Braziller, 1972: 79.

[21]Moss, 10.

[22]Georges Poulet, "Proust and Human Time." *Proust: A Collection of Critical Essays,* ed. René Girard, op. cit.: 177; Shattuck, 31-32; Deleuze, 48.

[23]Macksey, 111.

[24]*RTP* (Kilm) I: 261.

[25]*RTP* (Kilm) I: 377.

[26]*RTP* (Kilm) I: 410.

[27]*RTP* (Kilm) I: 413.

[28]*RTP* (Kilm) I: 435.

[29]*RTP* (Kilm) I: 438.

[30]*RTP* (Kilm) III: 656-57.

[31]*RTP* (Kilm) I: 415.

[32]Deleuze, 48; Germaine Brée, *Marcel Proust and Deliverance from Time,* trans. C. J. Richards and A. D. Truitt, New York: Grove Press, 1955: 235.

[33]This spatial rhythm linking perspective and the writer's point of view is another rhythm that recurs throughout *Remembrance of Things Past.* See Moss, 87-103; Poulet, 175; Nancy Lane "From Saint-Hilaire to Martinville and Beyond: Self, Desire, and Writing in *Remembrance of Things Past,*" *Style* 22 (1988): 391-401; Linda A. Gordon, "The Martinville Steeplechase: Charting the Course," *Style* 22 (1988): 402-09.

[34]*RTP* (Kilm) I: 147. This is in itself an interesting biological metaphor uniting time and space that is probably appropriate given the emergence of right and left brain differences and the probable multi-localization of memory.

[35]Deleuze, 112 ff.

[36]Deleuze, 149; Roger Shattuck, *Proust's Binoculars: A Study of Memory, Time, and Recognition in "A la recherche du temps perdu."* New York: Random House, 1963: 123.

[37]Brée, 222.

[38]Deleuze, 68.

[39]Poulet, 172.

[40]Richard Bernstein, "Howard's Way," *New York Times Magazine,* September 25, 1988: 41-44, 74, 92.

[41]Moss enumerates eighteen such examples, 97-99.

[42]Poulet, 160; Shattuck, *Marcel Proust,* 144.

[43]Brée, 224.

[44]*New York Times,* January 17, 1989, C9: 3.

[45]J.-F. Revel, *On Proust,* trans. Martin Turnell, New York: The Library Press, 1972: 14.

[46]Shattuck, following Proust's lead, posits that we all have this potential but only the artist undertakes the task to fashion a work of art out of his own experience. Shattuck, *Marcel Proust:* 164-65.

[47]Ibid., 127-35.

[48]Samuel Beckett, *Proust,* New York: Grove Press, 1931: 6-7.

[49]Nemerov, 116, 120.

[50]*RTP* (Kilm) I: 16.

[51]Marcel Proust, *Correspondance,* ed. Philip Kolb, Paris: Plon, 1984, tome XI, 1912: 286.

[52]Harvey, 21 (author's translation).

6

Proust's Referential Strategies and the Interrelations of the Liberal and Visual Arts

J. Theodore Johnson, Jr.

As any reader of *A LA RECHERCHE du temps perdu* knows, having encountered and then pondered about, the references to a church, a quartet, and the rivalry of François I and Charles V the Narrator thought he had *become* as the third sentence of the novel resolves, the richness of Proust's masterpiece emerges from strategies establishing elaborate cross-references between the fabric of his fictional texts, the real world, and the world of Art. While some may judge these references to be no more than airy embellishments thoughtlessly scattered across the surfaces of impressionistic prose, it is the view of this writer that Proust's references to the visual arts and their relations to our being in the real world constitute an intentional, integral part of the style of a man of vision, a bold, didactic Artist.

Emile Mâle opens the preface to his *L'Art religieux du XIIIe siècle en France* (a book Proust read soon after it appeared in 1898 and to which he later often refers in his translation of Ruskin, *La Bible d'Amiens*), with the statement: "Le Moyen Age a conçu l'art comme un enseignement."[1] Proust undoubtedly had in mind this classical idea of art pleasing and instructing as he set about constructing *cum pondere et mensura* as did Dante in his invisible fourteenth-century cathedral (cf. Mâle, p. 13) his own cathedral-novel. His Narrator refers to his work as "mes travaux d'architecte" as he wonders whether it would be understood: "je ne savais pas si ce serait une église où des fidèles sauraient peu à peu apprendre des vérités et découvrir des harmonies, le grand plan d'ensemble" (*RTP*, III, 1040).

As those who have worked with the manuscripts full well realize, Proust put together *A la recherche du temps perdu* with the thought and skill, scrupulous unto the smallest detail, of medieval Masters, artists, artisans, and masons collaborating in a common *chantier* and whose work, as did that of their classical predecessors—*Ars longa, vita brevis*—transforms physical reality along certain ideas into Art for the pleasure and instruction of generations of viewers and readers to come.

With geometrical rigor and joy, Proust placed the church of Saint-Hilaire at the center of Combray around which turns a circle with a 10-league radius drawn by a sentence 100 words long at the outset of *Combray II* (*RTP*, I, 48). And within walking distance out of that town which the remains of ramparts "cernait çà et là d'un trait aussi parfaitement circulaire qu'une petite ville dans un tableau de primitif," he built up the church Saint-André-des-Champs as a monument to chthonic French—such as Françoise or Robert de Saint-Loup—who more than stone structures, are the real *opus francigenum*:

> le véritable *opus francigenum,* dont le secret n'a pas été perdu depuis le
> XIIIe siècle, et qui ne périrait pas avec nos églises, ce ne sont pas tant
> les anges de pierre de Saint-André-des-Champs que les petits Français,
> nobles, bourgeois ou paysans, au visage sculpté avec cette délicatesse et
> cette franchise restées aussi traditionnelles qu'au porche fameux, mais
> encore créatrices. (*RTP,* II, 490)

It is for the delight and edification of his countrymen and the young, wandering *compagnons* whose intellectual route, knowing no borders, brings them to his *chantier* that Proust raised up a cathedral-novel. As the religious term "cathedral" designating an episcopal seat restricts the illuminating structures begun in the twelfth and designed to be carried out over into the thirteenth century at Amiens, Chartres, and Paris, so does, with Proust, the term novel. Proust's work, like the structures at Amiens, Chartres, and Paris, continues the classic tradition of the interrelations of the seven Liberal Arts under the aegis of Philosophy that stems from the Greece of the illuminating monuments of the Acropolis with the picture and statuary galleries of the Propylaea, the Parthenon, and Athena Nike and the thinking of Socrates, Plato, and Aristotle and continues to flourish in colleges and universities around the world. On the twelfth-century Romanesque western facade at Chartres, in the *voussures* surrounding the Nativity and the Virgin

and Child in majesty, figure the Liberal Arts consisting of the trivium—
Grammar, Rhetoric, and Dialectic—and the quadrivium—Geometry,
Arithmetic, Music, and Astronomy. Under the female allegorical personifi-
cations of each discipline are men who best represent each of the Liberal
Arts: the grammarian Donatus or Prisician, the rhetorician Cicero, the poly-
math dialectician Aristotle who founded the western world's second great
university in 335 B.C., the geometer Euclid, the mathematician Boethius,
the mathematician and musical theorist Pythagoras, and the astronomer
Ptolemy.[2]

After astronomy, and thus the completion of both the Bachelor and
Master of Arts, comes Philosophy. At the base of the central trumeau at
Notre-Dame in Paris, Viollet-le-Duc placed (cf. Aristotle next to Pisces and
Gemini at Chartres), Science next to Philosophy. Proust continues the tra-
dition of the interrelations of the Liberal and Visual Arts such as we find at
Chartres by weaving into the fabric of his text the philologist and professor
Brichot, the writer and philosopher Bergotte, the painter and art historian
Elstir, and the teacher and musician Vinteuil, along with a thorough understanding of modern science.[3] Emile Mâle has shown that a cathedral such
as Chartres synthesizes thirteenth-century knowledge in the same way as the
contemporary and encyclopedic *Speculum majus* of Vincent de Beauvais.
In the same fashion, Proust's *A la recherche du temps perdu* constitutes an
encyclopedic synthesis of his time. Time—and our place in it—beginning
with the opening sentence "Longtemps, je me suis couché de bonne heure"
until the novel's resolution placing itself "dans le Temps" concerns Proust
as it did the builders of Chartres.

Oriented towards the rising sun at the vernal equinox, which ends
the month of the infinitely expandable constellation of Pisces and begins the
month of Aries, the French cathedrals present to us at eye-level, as Ruskin
and Proust in *La Bible d'Amiens* (pp. 320-22) and Emile Mâle in the
chapter "Le Miroir de la Science" of *L'Art religieux du XIIIe siècle en
France* have admirably shown, stone zodiacs that mark out the twelve
months of the year and the rhythms of terrestrial works and days.[4] The
architecture and iconography also celebrate the ecclesiastical calendar: the
Feast of the Annunciation (March 25), the Feast of Saint John at the
summer solstice; the Feast of the Assumption of the Virgin into Heaven
(August 15), the Birth of Jesus (December 25), and Easter celebrated on the
first Sunday after the first full moon after the vernal equinox. Elstir, Marcel
Proust's fictional painter whose name combines the final letters of the

author's name with the ending of one of the three principal infinitive forms in French, and in the long tradition of the learned painter, explains at length for the adolescent Narrator during the important studio scene (*RTP*, I, 840-42) the iconography and vision of the medieval artists on the facade of the church at Balbec in a dense text several pages long that draws from Emile Mâle and from Proust's close analysis of the Bible and the churches and cathedrals of France.

Through discourse and art, Elstir brings the adolescent Narrator to consider wisdom: "On ne reçoit pas la sagesse, il faut la découvrir soi-même après un trajet que personne ne peut faire pour nous, ne peut nous épargner, car elle est un point de vue sur les choses" (*RTP*, I, 864). In this studio scene Proust brings the reader to an awareness of the Platonic distinctions between imagining, believing, thinking, and intellect, and as the various Liberal Arts interrelate philosophically on the facades of French cathedrals, so does Proust interrelate the teaching of the various representatives of the arts, and thus the philologist Brichot builds on the lessons of Elstir with the famous *Gnothi seauton*, "Know thyself," which he ascribes to Socrates (*RTP*, II, 1051-52).

The greatest literary masterpiece being but an alphabet in disorder, it behooves the philologist to consider the very elements of literature, a point John Ruskin makes in *Sesame and the Lilies* in a sentence Proust not only translated but set into relief with a footnote: "Et c'est pourquoi, avant tout, je vous dis instamment (je *sais* que j'ai raison en ceci): vous devez prendre l'habitude de regarder aux mots avec intensité et en vous assurant de leur signification syllabe par syllabe, plus, lettre par lettre."[5] Several pages later, in a text Proust also translated and highlighted with a footnote, Ruskin urges his readers to learn the Greek alphabet:

> Si vous ne savez pas l'alphabet grec, apprenez-le, jeune ou vieux, fille ou garçon, qui que vous puissiez être; si vous avez l'intention de lire sérieusement (ce qui naturellement implique que vous ayez quelque loisir à votre disposition), apprenez votre alphabet grec, ayez ensuite de bons dictionnaires de toutes ces langues et si jamais vous avez des doutes sur un mot, allez à la recherche avec une patience de chasseur.[6]

The elemental reading that Ruskin and Proust promote is quintessential in order to understand the Greek of the New Testament of the first century or the Latin of Horace who, in the penultimate decade prior to the new era, in lines 361-65 of *Ars poetica,* a work interrelating Liberal and Visual Arts, synthesizes *pictura* (surfaces) and *poesis* (making) of Art in five dactylic hexameters that expand a circle by five degrees to admit the annual threshold of a new year ever dawning:

> Ut pictura poesis: erit quae, si propius stes,
> te capiat magis, et quaedam, si longius abstes.
> haec amat obscurum, volet haec sub luce videri,
> iudicis argutum quae non formidat acumen;
> haec placuit semel, haec deciens repetita placebit.[7]

The elemental rigor of Horace's brilliant *Ars poetica* that begins with the word *Humano* and resolves, 111 lines after line 365, with *nisi plena cruoris, hirudo* is consonant with a great many texts by Proust. For "Une Enquête littéraire" published in *La Renaissance politique, littéraire, artistique* of 22 July 1922, Proust composed, just months before his death, a stunning *ars poetica* cast in the classical style of Horace as an arc of 180 words whose seventh and final sentence, "On n'a pas trop de toutes ses forces de soumission au réel, pour arriver à faire passer l'impression la plus simple en apparence du monde de l'invisible dans celui si différent du concret où l'ineffable se résout en claires formules,"[8] continues the tradition of *ostinato rigore* of Leonardo and the Renaissance.

This sort of rigor which demands that one master the elements of one's discipline and interrelate the Liberal Arts ranging from grammar to astronomy in order to understand visual arts and the world is simply beyond Swann who contents himself with surfaces. He has not dealt closely with texts and with iconography as has the Narrator who has heard, for example, Elstir's explanation of elements of the facade of the Balbec church: "Et l'ange qui emporte le soleil et la lune devenus inutiles puisqu'il est dit que la Lumière de la Croix sera sept fois plus puissante que celle des astres" (*RTP,* I, 841; cf. Rev. 21 : 23 which Elstir interprets fairly loosely), and thus he is at as much of a loss as those who believe the sun goes around the world or accept the paradigm "sun is to day as moon is to night" without thinking about a lunation, or month, the elements of our alphabet, and the goddess of the moon, Diana, and her twin brother, Apollo.

With the mathematical rigor that underlies the moving sweep of a Bach fugue, Proust sets into relief the lunacy of love-struck Swann in a brilliant paragraph in which he has Swann decide to work on Vermeer's

Diane et ses nymphes (*RTP*, I, 353-55). The paragraph consists of eleven sentences, eight of which, in terms of numbers of words, correspond either to a quarter of the moon or seven days, or multiples thereof, or to lunation (29 days, 12 hours, 44 minutes, and 2.8 seconds, but Proust understandably rounds off the figure to 29 days), giving the following pattern: sentence one, seven words or a week; sentences two and three, twenty-nine words each or two lunations; sentence four, fourteen words or two weeks; sentences five and ten, sixty-six and nine respectively; sentences six and eight, each with twenty-eight words or four weeks, surround sentence seven with thirty-eight words; sentences nine and eleven, with two hundred twenty-one and one hundred twenty-seven words respectively total three hundred and forty-eight words or exactly twelve lunations, or a lunar year. In other words, Proust interrelates the precision of astronomy, mathematics, and music—the final three sentences are typical of Proust's grand fugal writing—of the quadrivium with the verbal arts of the trivium along the lines of traditional iconography in the visual arts, and he does this with the calculated intentionality of the medieval architects who built twelve stone columns radiating out from a central circle of glass scalloped with twelve lunettes in the great rose windows on the western and northern facades of Notre-Dame at Chartres.

The second sentence of this paragraph with its twenty-nine words establishes the movement of the phases of the moon (one might think in this respect of a right to left movement of the first quarter as D and the waning crescent as C in the alphabet) by presenting the names of the cities to which Swann must travel in order to pursue his research on Vermeer in reverse alphabetical order, moving from the eighth to the second letter: "il aurait eu besoin de retourner au moins quelques jours à la Haye, à Dresde, à Brunswick," but in counterpoint to the moon, the phrase "au moins quelques jours" reminds us of the constant blaze of the sun. Proust introduces Diana in the third sentence, which like its predecessor, also consists of twenty-nine words: "Il était persuadé qu'une 'toilette de Diane' qui avait été achetée par le Mauritshuis à la vente Goldschmidt comme un Nicolas Maes, était en réalité de Ver Meer." But like Endymion sleeping before Selene, Swann goes no further into the matter than a dream: "Un jour il rêva qu'il partait pour un an; penché à la portière du wagon vers un jeune homme qui sur le quai lui disait adieu en pleurant, Swann cherchait à le convaincre de partir avec lui." And so when the jolt of the train wakes him up, Swann falls back into the lunar rhythms of the text, remembering "qu'il verrait Odette ce soir-là, le lendemain et presque chaque jour."

Through the referential strategies that form the underpinnings of this paragraph Proust incites the reader to think about the interrelations of the Liberal Arts from the elements of grammar through astronomy, and at the same time, since Swann quickly abandons the project, to examine for ourselves, a task made easier by good detailed reproductions, Vermeer's *Diana and the Nymphs*. Diana turns out to be a plump young woman with horns of a crescent moon bound by a filet in her hair and attended by four bored women in a sunny landscape under the watchful eye of a large black and white dog. And thus Vermeer and Proust seem to be dealing with what might be called a Diana complex, that bizarre aberration of events where earth and sun orbit an inconstant moon producing both astronomical and amorous disasters making it impossible for Swann to "quitter Paris pendant qu'Odette y était" (*RTP*, I, 353).

Nymphs orbiting Dianas appear before the adolescent Narrator pursuing Albertine at Balbec and who finds the French bourgeoisie to be "un atelier merveilleux de la sculpture la plus variée" from which "étaient issues ces Dianes et ces nymphes" (*RTP*, I, 844), and later the aristocratic Princesse de Guermantes passes by "belle et légère comme Diane" (*RTP*, II, 56). Yet the concept of Diana as lunar huntress surrounded by nymphs and eschewing men is a chilling one indeed, for it corroborates the quotations from Alfred de Vigny's "La Colère de Samson" at the outset of *Sodome et Gomorrhe*: "La femme aura Gomorrhe et l'homme aura Sodome" (*RTP*, II, 601) and "les deux sexes mourront chacun de son côté" in the immense sentence, the longest in the novel, that deals with homosexuality (*RTP*, II, 615-18). Two paragraphs prior to that sentence, Proust has Charlus speak about his failure to bed a certain *chasseur:*

> J'ai su depuis qu'il n'avait jamais eu aucune de mes lettres, qui avait été interceptées, la première par le garçon d'étage qui était envieux, la seconde par le concierge de jour qui était vertueux, la troisième par le concierge de nuit qui aimait le jeune chasseur [the Ms has "la jeune chasseresse"] et couchait avec lui à l'heure où Diane se levait. (*RTP*, II, 613)

Proust, ever concerned with the theme and variations around our conceptions of time, casts this material into sixty-one words (cf. the first minute after an hour) complete with spatial references (the *garçon d'étage*) and circadian rhythms of the hotel with the opposition of the virtuous *concierge de jour* and the venal *concierge de nuit*. The proximity of the word *chasseur* (word 50) to Diana (word 59) heightens the grandly baroque, Charlusian resonances of the sentence.

In *Le Temps retrouvé,* in a sentence consonant with line 365 of Horace's *Ars poetica* which completes the circle of the year and the ever-present question of judgment—*haec placuit semel, haec deciens repetita placebit*—Proust speculates as to what posterity will retain of "our" time:

> La poésie d'un élégant foyer et de belles toilettes de notre temps ne se trouvera-t-elle pas plutôt, pour la postérité, dans le salon de l'éditeur Charpentier par Renoir que dans le portrait de la princesse de Sagan ou de la comtesse de La Rochefoucauld par Cotte ou Chaplin? (*RTP,* III, 722)

The Renoir and Chaplin portraits are both dated 1878. In the former we see Mme Charpentier and her daughters while a very large dog sprawls out on the grid of a very simple but elegant Asian rug, and in the latter, an elegant woman rises out of swirling clouds of cloth in the grand manner of Belle Epoque baroque to arrest us as we orbit by her lovely gaze. Her left hand fingers the folds over her bosom out of which arches a long strand of pearls that swings around the left side of her neck, and a perky aigrette tops her coiffure out of which rises the crescent moon of Diana.[9]

Swann, rapt in surface reflections, glides over reality and thus remains as the Narrator eventually discovers, "en deçà de l'art" (*RTP,* I, 852). Oblivious to more engaging ideas, Swann inevitably focuses on inconsequential surface detail, and thus he recognizes "sous les couleurs d'un Ghirlandajo, le nez de M. de Palancy" (*RTP,* I, 223). Proust makes the reference general so that the reader might recall any number of paintings by Ghirlandajo (1449-94) in which figures a male nose. And a brief search inevitably produces the painting in the Louvre of an *Old Man and His Grandson* where the two, both in vital reds, look at each other within a grey, abstract structure pierced with the right angle of a window without top and right side that reveals a path and a river, a chapel beyond nestled entirely under a hill smaller than the rocky mount in the distance which, like Gibraltar or Jebel Musa, marks out an obstacle to surmount and a portal to new worlds.

In the new century, the young boy will have grown old and will gaze into the clear eyes of a young man into whose hands will be passed yet again the world. Each man must know the world anew. Proust's Narrator becomes Adam in the fourth paragraph of the novel. In the fifth paragraph with its three hundred and sixty words distributed in five sentences beginning "Un homme qui dort tient en cercle autour de lui le fil des heures, l'ordre des années et des mondes," Proust pushes human consciousness back into primitive, animal being before cavemen, to then draw it up into the present and awareness of the *moi*.

In the twenty-fourth of the thirty-eight paragraphs after the initial nine of *Combray I* and which is part of the *drame du coucher,* the Narrator sees himself before his father as Isaac before Abraham:

> Je restai sans oser faire un mouvement; il était encore devant nous, grand, dans sa robe de nuit blanche sous le cachemire de l'Inde violet et rose qu'il nouait autour de sa tête depuis qu'il avait des névralgies, avec le geste d'Abraham dans la gravure d'après Benozzo Gozzoli que m'avait donnée M. Swann, disant à Sarah qu'elle a à se départir du côté d'Isaac.
> (*RTP,* I, 36-37)

Readers who take seriously the precept promoted by Ruskin and Proust about looking at a text word by word and letter by letter and to know the Greek alphabet will appreciate the rigor with which Proust has constructed this paragraph and this particular sentence with its seventy-two words and nineteen *i*'s, of which two are capitalized: *Inde and Isaac.* Veiled though may be Endymion's night, the light of dawn inevitably follows a sleepless night (*robe de nuit blanche*). What hiding (*cacher*) but what seeing (*mirer*) in *le cachemire* from the East from whence rises the sun whose ever-clearing predawn colors Homeric Proust specifies (*violet et rose*) in a poetic strategy that weaves Old Testament *pictura* through New Testament *poesis* to produce a sentence, a single thread, that recalls the genealogy of Jesus as descending directly from Isaac and Abraham as spelled out in the Greek both in the opening lines of Matthew 1 : 1-16 and again in Luke 3 : 23-38.

Although there is an engraving by Ruskin after Benozzo Gozzoli of *Abraham Parting from the Angels* in the Library Edition of *Modern Painters* (Volume IV, plate 10, after p. 316 of Chapter V, "Of the Superhuman Ideal"), and there were scenes from the life of Abraham in the now-destroyed Campo Santo in Pisa, it would seem likely that Proust has

invented both the biblical incident and this particular work by Benozzo
Gozzoli.[10] But if the searches of the curious reader for the specific engraving made after a work by Gozzoli relevant to this particular scene in the life
of Abraham and Isaac are, in the end, fruitless, what abundance along the
way when one inevitably falls upon the brilliant *Procession of the Magi.*
Here Gozzoli, in frescoes executed for the Medici chapel in Florence,
joyously illuminates Matthew 2 : 1 where an unspecified number of Magi
come from the east to seek out the Christ Child by placing mounted, full-
length portraits of the principal Medici males in the foreground of the walls
while behind them are scores of men of every age, race, and station caught
on their way to Bethlehem to see the Infant Jesus. These men, all triumph-
antly vital in the sumptuous dress of the Renaissance, meet our passing gaze
in the present.[11]

The Virgin and Child in Andrea Mantegna's magnificent San Zeno
altarpiece are surrounded by nine cherubs, and in each of the flanking side
panels of this triptych stand four saints: Saints Zeno, John the Evangelist,
Paul and Peter on the Virgin's right, and Saints Benedict, Lawrence,
Gregory Nazianzen, and John the Baptist. Proust strategically brings this
extraordinary work to our attention through what appears to be a rather
casual reference. When Swann mounts the stairs to the Sainte-Euverte
soirée, he sees a *grand gaillard en livrée* and draws his usual connections
between the surfaces of reality and art:

> Il semblait précisément appartenir à cette race disparue—ou qui peut-être
> n'exista jamais que dans le retable, de San Zeno et les fresques des
> Eremitani où Swann l'avait approchée et où elle rêve encore—issue de
> la fécondation d'une statue antique par quelque modèle padouan du
> Maître ou quelque Saxon d'Albert Dürer.[12]

As with other references to works of music and art, Proust gently urges us
to view Mantegna's San Zeno altarpiece for ourselves, and, discovering no
equivalent of a *grand gaillard en livrée,* to deploy the deep gaze required to
go beyond the surface *pictura* to enter through *poesis* into that zone where
the painting becomes, as Leonardo puts it, *cosa mentale* (*RTP,* II, 1190).

Of the eight saints flanking the Virgin and Child, only one does not
hold or read a book. Across from young Saint John the Evangelist who
intently reads his book, young Saint Lawrence, palm in right hand and left
hand resting on a grill, gazes out of the luminous atmosphere of the classical

pavilion Mantegna has created for his composition and into light from beyond, a world of dark blue sky and white clouds. The attitudes of the two young saints recall those of the two students under the figure of Grammatica on the western portal of Notre-Dame of Chartres, and the classical medallions with horses, centaurs, and men on either side of the Virgin's head recall certain friezes on the inner wall of the Parthenon.

Directly under the coffered ceiling courses a very evident band of eggs and darts whose marmoreal chill sets into relief the joyous swags of greens into which have been lovingly woven vegetables, fruits, and nuts from various seasons so that acorns and apricots mingle with beans and cherries, very much in the spirit of the tree of life rendering its fruit each according to the twelve months (Rev. 22 : 2), and the swags are gathered up together in the center of the composition by a ring from which hangs a golden disk separating a large ostrich egg from the small flame of a votive lamp, a compositional detail and iconographic motif greatly simplified in the *Brera Altarpiece* by Piero della Francesca.[13]

Birth, death, and life, as in Mantegna's painting, are beautifully celebrated in the Combray in which Léonie lives and dies. The poetic rigor of Proust in his prose, like Hesiod for Greece and Virgil for Italy in their poems, celebrates France and our world from a certain perspective. One need not to have contemplated the Ionic order with its fluted columns and eggs and darts between the infinitely spiraling volutes on the temple of Athena Nike to understand the French proverb *On ne fait pas d'omelette sans casser les œufs*. So if the young Narrator, on the one hand, is repulsed by the sight of Françoise killing a chicken, on the other hand he relishes the perspective of that same chicken brought to table "sa peau brodée d'or comme une chasuble et son jus précieux égoutté d'un ciboire" (*RTP*, I, 122).

Along similar lines, the perfect circle that one hundred words circumscribe in a ten-league radius around medieval Combray at the outset of Combray is necessarily bisected by the modern railroad over which move speeding trains whose schedules do not coincide with the bells of Saint-Hilaire and which bring to the town the Narrator and his parents at the vernal equinox during the week before Easter. The Narrator's father, always quick to see beautiful geometries in the world, for it is he who points out the circular shadows cast by apple trees and later moves his cane through the slanted shafts of golden afternoon light as they sift through the tree's leaves (*RTP*, I, 146), is the first to see the little iron rooster on the top of Saint-

Hilaire run in circles in the furrows of the heavens: "mon père l'apercevait qui filait tour à tour sur tous les sillons du ciel, faisant courir en tous sens son petit coq de fer" (RTP, I, 63).

Similarly, Proust deploys the same strategies that involve the interrelations of the Liberal and Visual Arts when it comes to what is known in French as Le Jour de l'An and which, ten days after the winter solstice, occurs on January 1. One has to follow somewhat closely Proust's circular strategy in this particular case because it begins by establishing in the reader's mind connections between Giovanni Battista Piranesi's Rome in Vedute di Roma and what are really Proust's views of Paris in Du côté de chez Swann in a text where the Narrator tells us he knows a window from which one can see

> une cloche violette, parfois rougeâtre, parfois aussi, dans les plus nobles 'épreuves' qu'en tire l'atmosphère, d'un noir décanté de cendres, laquelle n'est autre que le dôme de Saint-Augustin et qui donne à cette vue de Paris le caractère de certaines vues de Rome par Piranesi.[14]

Amazed at the perspective of having to disrupt a father's rational division of the cartographic reality of Paris (so as to expedite, during the ritual visits, the distribution of the traditional marrons glacés on the Jour de l'An) in order to placate an avuncular idea of family precedence, the young Narrator, hard at work as a schoolboy learning the elements of the Liberal Arts, imagines, with the help of Proust who lays out with the precise strokes of Piranesi's burin, a trajectory that, criss-crossing Paris, would produce Vedute di Parigi worthy of the Italian master of the Enlightenment: "Cet oncle serait surement blessé; il n'eût trouvé que naturel que nous allassions de la Madeleine au Jardin des Plantes où il habitait, avant de nous arrêter à Saint-Augustin, pour repartir rue de l'Ecole-de-Médecine" (RTP, I, 486).

Beginning with the concept of a year as a ring upon which are marked out three hundred and sixty-five days of which one, Le Jour de l'An, is traditionally singled out to mark a new year's beginning, like birthdays, Proust views Paris in this instance as a grand circle on whose northern and southern points rise up Montmartre and Montparnasse and across which flows from east to west the arc of the river Seine. The geographic trajectory he describes runs northwest by southeast, just west of the center point on the Ile-de-la-Cité between Notre-Dame and the Palais de

Justice, but the intellectual territory (with strong biographical overtones) is immense, for it runs from an Empire structure named to honor the Magdalene before whom appeared the risen Christ as gardener to the garden as site of scientific analysis and documentation to Augustine of Hippo, one of the four Latin Fathers of the Church whose name graces a church in which Baltard used for the first time a metallic armature and which was completed in 1871, the year of Marcel Proust's birth, and it stops with the Rue de l'Ecole-de-Médecine with its Ecole de Médecine in which the writer's father, just before he was to preside over an examination at the nearby Faculté de Médecine, suffered an attack on Monday, 23 November 1903 and from which, never regaining consciousness, he died, at home, on Thursday, 26 November, 1903.[15]

A subtle and very moving tribute to his father, as are so many of the texts dealing with those Liberal Arts studied in the quadrivium along the lines of the scientific investigation that rises out of Aristotle and the university he founded, this text also constitutes a tribute to the collective genius of the architects who, over the centuries, built Paris. To connect the four points that Proust sets down, each reader must provide a mental itinerary. Does one go by foot over the Pont des Arts between the Louvre and its paintings and the Institut de France and the Académie Française or does one go by carriage over the Pont-Neuf that takes one from the biblical La Samaritaine into the Quai des Grands Augustins, taking first Saint-Michel and then Saint-Germain before encountering a sextet of streets with scientific names—Jussieu, Lacépède, Linné, Buffon, Cuvier, Geoffroy-Saint-Hilaire—that lead into or border the Jardin des Plantes. But in any case, to get to the Rue de l'Ecole-de-Médecine from Saint-Augustin one would most likely go through the *guichets* of the Louvre and then over the Pont du Carrousel to the Quai Voltaire before engaging oneself in the mass of streets and academic institutions of the Quartier Latin.

The references to the visual arts—architecture, painting, engraving, and urban planning—contribute to the color of the story as it develops on the level of *pictura,* yet when viewed through *poesis* and the interrelations of the seven Liberal Arts and Philosophy, these references, in the manner of grand, freely turning kaleidoscopes, bring us to confront in ever wider circles ourselves and the world through Art. The referential strategies deployed by Proust with impeccable style are also to be found in his non-fictional writings, such as his response published in *L'Opinion* of 28 February 1920, to an inquiry as to which eight French paintings in the collections of the Louvre he would propose to have exhibited in a "Tribune Française" as a pendant to the recently installed Italian Tribune.[16]

The response is typical of the rigor we expect from Proust: an arc of two sentences (180 words) that runs from *S* to *t* broken by the middle sentence consisting of sixteen words revolving around the idea of not turning a museum into "un hôtel Pagès quelconque" (*CSB*, p. 601). References to *L'Or du Rhin,* the first opera of Wagner's tetralogy *Der Ring des Nibelungen,* and to the last quartets of Beethoven prepare, with a large sweep, the terrain in which Proust will write about Art. Proust announces limiting himself to the specified eight paintings, but he then produces what appears hasty but is a quite thoughtful list naming seven painters, nine paintings, and implying a tenth:

> *Portrait of Chardin,* par lui-même; *Portrait de Mme Chardin* par Chardin; *Nature morte* de Chardin; *Le Printemps,* de Millet; *L'Olympia,* de Manet; un Renoir ou *La Barque du Dante,* ou *La Cathédrale de Chartres* de Corot; *L'Indifférent* de Watteau, ou *L'Embarquement.* (*CSB,* p. 601).

Proust begins his "Tribune Française" in the eighteenth century—the Age of Reason, the Enlightenment, and *Le Siècle des Lumières*—with Chardin's self-portrait and the portrait of his wife, two humans, male and female, each rendered in pastel on paper, a medium as ephemeral as the subjects and life itself. As all of Chardin's still lifes turn around human concerns and abstract ideas, Proust gently suggests to us by not making a selection that any of his works deserve close scrutiny and inclusion in the "Tribune Française." All choices are human and begin, like Proust's first selections, with male and female vibrantly alive and rational in the world.

After the exactingly orchestrated Romantic storms of Beethoven and Wagner, Millet's *Le Printemps* shows against a dark sky no longer menacing a rainbow's arc over a sun-drenched forested hill and worked fields with fruit trees whose round shadows, were this an illustration of spring in Combray, the Narrator's father would most likely have admired. *L'Olympia* by Manet moves beyond the child's world of Combray to the realities of Paris which Proust explores in the later novel as frontally as does Manet. The two Chardin pastel portraits form a couple; Manet's oil portrait of Olympia engages us as partner.

Here, then, is a handful of five pictures. How to move to the sixth? Proust proposed three alternatives: "Un Renoir, ou *La Barque du Dante,* ou *La Cathédrale de Chartres* de Corot." By including Renoir with the two nineteenth-century masters, Proust pays homage to a painter who had just recently died but whose vision of women he celebrates in 1920 in the preface to Paul Morand's *Tendres Stocks* and that is recast in *Le Côté de Guermantes II* (*RTP,* II, 327 and 1155-56) and that will appear in the following year. By not mentioning Eugène Delacroix as the painter of *La Barque du Dante,* Proust focuses attention on Dante and Virgil and the *katábasis* or elemental descent important also in Wagner and *L'Or du Rhin* if one is going to forge, like young Siegfried his sword, a ring.

With references to Dante and Chartres cathedral as painted by Corot, Proust renders homage to the generations of brilliant artists firmly committed to the classical tradition of the Liberal Arts which flowered in the literature and the architecture of the twelfth century. Corot's picture shows a young boy and a young girl resting by loosely piled ashlars before a large mound of grass-covered earth up from which grow several slim young trees on either side of a mounting path, and we are reminded, as the afternoon sun illuminates the western facade with the cycles of the seasons and the Liberal Arts, that the Cathedral of Chartres was built up stone upon stone over generations, and whose descendants, the real *opus francigenum,* like the children around Saint-André-des-Champs in Combray, are these youngsters. Will these children master the Liberal Arts in order to grow intellectually free, or will they be content to remain, even though they move freely about in the sun and enjoy the world constructed for their edification by their forefathers, in those mental operations that Plato identifies as imagining, believing, and even thinking that keep an individual in the cave?

What will the children before Corot's *La Cathédrale de Chartres* become as they move from late adolescence into young adulthood? Having begun in the Age of Reason with the portraits by Chardin of his wife and himself, both fairly on in years, Proust returns to the eighteenth century for his final selection for this "Tribune Française," one of two works by Antoine Watteau, *L'Indifférent* or *L'Embarquement.* How does one look at *L'Indifférent?* Are we the mirror into which the Indifferent One is looking? Are we the Indifferent One? Do we, like him, avoid reality and dream of sailing away, like those in *L'Embarquement,* to the never-never land of Cythera, or going, as Dorothy wistfully sings in *The Wizard of Oz,* "Somewhere over the rainbow?" By omitting the reference to Cythera in the usual title *L'Embarquement pour l'île de Cythère* or *Le Pèlerinage à l'isle de Cythère,* Proust reminds us that each individual embarks on an odyssey that may, or may not, lead—as Elstir puts it in *A l'ombre des jeunes filles en fleurs*—to "sagesse . . . un point de vue sur les choses."

Through masterfully deployed referential strategies, Proust encompasses, like the immense temporal circle of *un homme qui dort* in the fifth paragraph of the novel or the ten-league radius around Saint-Hilaire at the outset of *Combray II,* or the brilliant arc interrupted only by the intrusion of a "Hôtel Pagès quelconque" into a projected "Tribune Française," the immense richness of life as it is revealed to us through Art. Whatever the ostensible subject matter of a painting may be and however sensitive that subject may be to some, the overriding concern of Proust is to bring these illuminating works by Masters of times past into the present of our own lives that we might look deeply into them to discover, as our gaze adjusts to such depths, a certain unmistakable gleam—call it happiness—radiating out from the work. Proust knowingly and urgently refers to these works so that his readers will discover—and not without the inevitable risks of an odyssey—"sagesse . . . un point de vue sur les choses." Like Homer, Virgil, and Dante, Proust epically transformed life into Art.

Notes

[1]*L'Art religieux du XIIIe siècle en France*, 2 vols. (Paris: Armand Colin, 1958) 1: 11, or see the Dora Nussey translation, *The Gothic Image: Religious Art in France of the Thirteenth Century* (New York: Harper & Row, 1972) vii. Marcel Proust's translation of John Ruskin, *La Bible d'Amiens*, was republished by Mercure de France in 1947. References to *A la recherche du temps perdu* are to the edition by Pierre Clarac and André Ferré (Paris: Gallimard [Bibliothèque de la Pléiade], 1954).

[2]Both Emile Mâle's chapter "Le Miroir de la Science" in *L'Art religieux du XIIIe siècle en France*: 157-83 and the photographs of Etienne Houvet in his *Cathédrale de Chartres: Portail occidental ou royal XIIe siècle* (Chelles: A. Faucheux, 1919) are indispensable for an understanding of how the Liberal Arts and Philosophy interrelate with the Visual Arts in the sculptured program of the facade. As the Narrator discovers in *A l'Ombre des jeunes filles en fleurs*, it is helpful to study the casts in the Musée des Monuments Français in Paris (*RTP*, I, 659) before going to the sites. On Proust and architecture, see Richard Bales, *Proust and the Middle Ages* (Genève: Droz, 1975), Kay Bourlier, *Marcel Proust et l'architecture* (Montréal: Les Presses de l'Université de Montréal, 1980), and my article "Marcel Proust and Architecture: Some Thoughts on the Cathedral-Novel," in *Critical Essays on Marcel Proust*, ed. Barbara J. Bucknall (Boston: G. K. Hall & Co., 1987) 133-61. The fine painting by the fifteenth-century Florentine Francesco Pesellino of the *Seven Liberal Arts* in the Birmingham Museum of Art (Birmingham, Alabama) and which includes *Arismetrica* and *Rethorica* in the flanks around central *Astro* (part of a circle of stars) *logia* may have stimulated, as it must still, many a lively discussion.

[3]In addition to Sandra S. Beyer, "The Sciences in the Works of Marcel Proust," diss., University of Kansas, 1973, see John D. Erickson, "The Proust-Einstein Relation: A Study in Relative Point of View" in *Marcel Proust: A Critical Panorama*, ed. Larkin B. Price (Urbana: U of Illinois P, 1973) 247-76, and William C. Carter, "Proust, Einstein, et le sentiment religieux cosmique," *Bulletin de la Société des Amis de Marcel Proust et des Amis de Combray* 37 (1987) 52-62.

[4]Orientation is a constant concern in architecture. At the summer solstice the sun descends below the plane halfway between the pyramids of Khufu and Khafre (see Dora Jane Hamblin, "Unlocking the secrets of the Giza Plateau," *Smithsonian* 17: 1 [April 1986] 93). In Birmingham, Alabama, the earth's turning causes the morning sunlight to cast changing designs over the personnifications of Power, Light, and Heat on the facade of the Alabama Power Building, and Vulcan's constant nocturnal embrace, between mind and hand, of the North Star, is consonant with the vigil of the memorial Campanile on Mount Oread of the University of Kansas.

[5]John Ruskin, *Sésame et les lys*. Traduction et Notes de Marcel Proust, Précédé de *Sur la lecture* de Marcel Proust. Edition établie par Antoine Compagnon (Bruxelles:

Editions Complexe [Coll. Le Regard littéraire] 1987) 138. The implications of the myth of Io and the origin of the Greek alphabet and their interrelations with the Liberal Arts and the other Arts under Apollo have been brilliantly set out by Geoffroy Tory in his *Champ fleury* (Paris: A Lenseigne du Pot Casse par Maistre Geofroy Tory de Bourges / Libraire & Autheur du dict Livre. Et par Giles Gourmont aussi Libraire demourant en la Rue sainct Iaques a Lenseigne des Trois Couronnes [1529]). This indispensable book has been reprinted with an introduction, notes, index, and glossary by Gustave Cohen (Paris: Charles Bosse, 1931), and there is a reprint of the original edition with introduction by J. W. Jolliffe (New York: Johnson Reprint Corp., 1970). It has been translated into English and annotated by George B. Ines as *Champ fleury* (New York: The Grolier Club, 1927). A related work is Albrecht Dürer, *On the Just Shaping of Letters*, translated by R. T. Nichol from the Latin text of the edition of MDXXXV (New York: Dover, 1965).

[6]*Sésame* 151. *Cratylus* and *Theaetetus*, two Socratic dialogues by Plato, corroborate Ruskin and the descent into the elements of literature. In the Psychomachia on the facade of Notre-Dame of Amiens, *Patience* and *Colère* are found under Saint André (see Ruskin/Proust, *La Bible d'Amiens* 291 and Mâle 123-24). For the general question of the Virtues and Vices, see my article "Proust and Giotto: Foundations for an Allegorical Interpretation of *A la recherche du temps perdu*" in *Marcel Proust: A Critical Panorama*, ed. Larkin B. Price (Urbana: U of Illinois P., 1973) 168-205. This tradition of the Psychomachia is continued by Francesco Pesellino in the pendant to his *Seven Liberal Arts, The Seven Virtues*, in the Birmingham Museum of Art (Birmingham, Alabama) and which is reproduced in George Ferguson, *Signs and Symbols in Christian Art* (New York: Oxford U P, 1961) Pl. 60. The hunt figures conspicuously on twelfth- and thirteenth-century church facades. See Jean Villette, "La Chasse vue par les imagiers de la cathédrale," in *Notre-Dame de Chartres*, 1: 4 (Octobre-Novembre, 1970) 17-19. Cf. "Les Phares" where Baudelaire sees art as "Un appel de chasseurs perdus dans les grands bois" and Pieter Breughel the Elder's *The Return of the Hunters* (Kunsthistorisches Museum, Vienna). In the middle of the dinner party in *Le Côté de Guermantes* Proust's narrator goes on a hunt that puts all of the Guermantes into a heavy romanesque structure with very few windows in the text that begins "avec la même joie qu'un homme qui, perdu dans une forêt, lit au bout de deux flèches, disposées en sens contraire sur une plaque indicatrice et suivies d'un chiffre fort petit de kilomètres: 'Belvédère Casimir-Perier' et 'Croix du Grand-Veneur', et comprend par là qu'il est dans le bon chemin" (*RTP*, II, 534).

[7]Horace, *Satires, Epistles, Ars Poetica*, with an English Translation by H. Rushton Fairclough (London and New York: The Loeb Classical Library, 1926) 480. One possible rendering of the text: "So painting poetry: there will be such a one that, should you stand closer, / might capture you more, and another, if you should stand away farther. / This one loves shade; intends this one under light to be seen, / the bright acumen of the judge fears this one not; / this one pleased once, this one tens of times over will please." For the tradition surrounding *ut pictura poesis* and the arts, see

Rensselaer W. Lee's indispensable study *Ut Pictura Poesis: The Humanistic Theory of Painting* (New York: W. W. Norton & Co., 1967).

[8]*Contre Sainte-Beuve* précédé de *Pastiches et mélanges* et suivi de *Essais et articles*, ed. établie par Pierre Clarac avec la collaboration d'Yves Sandre (Paris: Gallimard [Bibliothèque de la Pléiade], 1971) 645.

[9]Proust writes about this portrait in "Le Salon de la comtesse Aimery de La Rochefoucauld" first published by Philip Kolb and Larkin Price in *Textes retrouvés* (Urbana: U of Illinois P, 1968) 38-41. See also *Correspondance de Marcel Proust*, ed. Philip Kolb (Paris: Plon, 1981), 8 (1908) 21.

[10]Albert Mingelgrün in *Thèmes et structures bibliques dans l'œuvre de Marcel Proust* (Lausanne: L'Age d'Homme, 1978) 94 follows Marcel Gutwirth in noting that the episode does not figure in the Bible nor in known works by Gozzoli.

[11]The Narrator discourses on Swann's *manie* of identifying people he knows in painting and develops the idea of anachronism both in the Benozzo Gozzoli cortege of the Magi fifteen centuries after the Nativity and the four centuries that then separate these frescoes from Swann (*RTP*, I, 535). In playful symmetry, Proust has Swann fall in love with Odette because she looks like Zipporah, daughter of Jethro (and who becomes the wife of Moses) in the Botticelli fresco in the Sistine Chapel in the Vatican (*RTP*, I, 222-23, 225, and 238), and after their marriage and the birth of their child, Gilberte, Odette becomes Botticelli's *Virgin of the Magnificat* (*RTP*, I, 617-18). The section of this painting to which Proust refers where the Virgin dips "sa plume dans l'encrier que lui tend l'ange, avant d'écrire sur le livre saint où est déjà tracé le mot 'Magnificat' " (*RTP*, I, 618) has been reproduced in Gabriele Mandel, *Tout l'œuvre peint de Botticelli* (Paris: Flammarion, 1968) Pl. XXVII facing Pl. XXVI which reproduces the tondo.

[12]*RTP*, I, 324. A splendid reproduction of the San Zeno altarpiece at Verona is to be found in *Mantegna*, No. 95 of the series *Chefs-d'œuvre de l'art: Grands Peintres* (9 au 16 avril 1968) Pl. II-III. The Louvre *Saint Sebastian* (Pl. VIII), one of the likely models for Legrandin as Saint Sebastian of snobism, deserves much more thought than surface identifications in the manner of Swann. A close analysis of Dürer's great triptych that opens with *Knight, Death, and the Devil* (1513) and *Saint Jerome in His Study* (1514) puts the third, *Melancholia I* (1514), into a certain relief. Proust's strategy in these references to works by Mantegna and Dürer is precisely to urge us into looking deeply into the thoughtful works by these two Renaissance Masters.

[13]See Pl. LXIV in *The Complete Paintings of Piero della Francesca*, notes and catalogue by Pierluigi de Vecchi in the series Penguin Classics of World Art (New York: Penguin Books, 1985). On the back cover is a statement by John Berger about Piero della Francesca that could also apply to Proust: "He is the supreme painter of *knowledge*. As acquired through the methods of science or—and this makes more sense than seems likely—as acquired through happiness."

[14]*RTP*, I, 66. Of the numerous possibilities, and indeed all of the *Vedute di Roma* merit close analysis, one might select Pl. I, *Veduta della Piazza del Popolo* in

Magnificenza di Roma nelle vedute di Giovanni Battista Piranesi, con una introduzzione di Mario Praz e note illustrative di Livio Jannatoni (Milano: Edizioni Il Polifilo, 1961). Comparison of this engraving with a photograph of the site as seen today in the last plate (41) in Herschel Levit, *Views of Rome Then and Now: 41 Etchings by Giovanni Battista Piranesi and Corresponding Photographs and Text* (New York: Dover, 1978) sets into relief the Art of the eighteenth-century architect. Proust's single reference to Piranesi's *Views of Rome,* when pursued, can open up illuminating perspectives on both Rome and Paris.

[15]In the zodiac on the western facade of Chartres is the sculpture of January (Janus). The young man who will grow into a man looks, for the moment, in not quite the opposite direction of the mature man in this bicephalic sculpture. Eventually, as in the Ghirlandajo portrait of the old man and the boy, the young man will become the mature adult whose large knife cuts up through and towards himself the round, traditional—in this case double-layered—*galette* of the New Year. See Pl. 33 of Houvet and his caption: "Le mois de Janvier, homme à deux têtes: un vieillard l'année écoulée, un jeune homme l'année nouvelle, il coupe le gâteau des rois" (Portail royal XIIe siècle). How not to see Proust's splendid New Year's text as a tribute to his father, as is the sculpture on Notre-Dame of Chartres to fathers and sons, to whom he dedicated *La Bible d'Amiens: "A la mémoire de mon père, frappé en travaillant le 24 novembre 1903 mort le 26 novembre cette traduction est tendrement dédiée"* [5]. The beautiful portrait of *Le Professeur Adrien Proust* by Jean Lecomte du Noüy figured, along with the portrait of *Madame Adrien Proust* by Charles Landelle, in the exhibition of portraits organized by Professor Heather McPherson in the Visual Arts Gallery of the University of Alabama at Birmingham in 1988 and for which she prepared the informative catalog *Fin-de-Siècle Faces: Portraiture in the Age of Proust, 25 September-20 November, 1988* (Birmingham, Alabama: The University of Alabama at Birmingham, 1988). In academic attire, the man whom we now know as Marcel Proust's father is portrayed as a man of science with feather pen poised over papers, much like Aristotle as teacher and writer in the Liberal Arts cycle at Chartres, and his candid and frank gaze meets ours over time (the sands of his hour-glass are arrested in the painting; but as Proust's New Year's text in his honor reminds us as it traces the great cartographic circle of Paris, the Seine always flows on to the sea).

[16]Proust mentions over two hundred painters in his writings. The following fully documented studies provide extensive bibliographic references and contribute to our understanding of Proust and painting: Helen O. Borowitz, "Visions of Moreau in Huysmans and Proust" and "The Watteau and Chardin of Marcel Proust," in *The Impact of Art on French Literature from De Scudéry to Proust* (Newark: U of Delaware P, 1985) 147-65 and 166-88; J. M. Cocking, "Proust and Painting," in *Proust: Collected Essays on the Writer and His Art* (Cambridge: Cambridge U P, 1982) 130-63; and my article "Proust and Painting" in *Critical Essays on Marcel Proust,* ed. Barbara J. Bucknall Boston: G. K. Hall, 1987) 162-80.

7

Les Rééditions de Proust

Jean Milly

L'ÉVÉNEMENT LITTÉRAIRE DE LA RENTRÉE 1987 en France a été la réédition, par plusieurs éditeurs en même temps, d'*A la recherche du temps perdu*. Le fait a pu étonner, et pour plusieurs raisons. D'abord, on croyait avec une tranquille certitude que l'on possédait depuis trente-trois ans l'édition infaillible et définitive que Clarac et Ferré avaient établie pour la Bibliothèque de la Pléiade, à partir des manuscrits qu'ils avaient pu consulter. Elle remplaçait une édition originale peu satisfaisante, et pouvait se parer de nombreux avantages de sérieux et de correction, mais aussi d'une grande maniabilité, de résumés, d'index, d'introductions et de notes d'apparat critique. Elle avait été adoptée par tous les critiques et chercheurs comme l'unique édition de référence. Alors, pourquoi donc remettre en question un instrument commode et commun, au risque de troubler lecteurs et même spécialistes? Pourquoi multiplier les textes et les présentations? Le livre allait-il devenir une nouvelle Bible, dont le commentaire et la lettre même étaient destinés à varier selon les dogmes et les sectes entre lesquels se partageraient les fidèles?

Ne poussons pourtant pas trop loin le parallèle avec l'exégèse religieuse, si mystique que Proust ait pu paraître à certains. En fait, cette apparente bousculade sur les traces de Proust correspondait à la date du passage de la grande œuvre dans le domaine public, c'est-à-dire que la propriété littéraire cessait, à partir de ce moment, d'appartenir à ses héritiers, et que l'édition du livre cessait d'être réservée à un seul éditeur, à savoir Gallimard. L'événement avait un caractère éditorial, juridique et, on le verra, proprement littéraire. Il était de l'intérêt de Gallimard de se présenter comme le garant de la continuité, de l'héritage familial, autrement dit de la tradition et presque du dogme, tandis que d'autres éditeurs se disposaient à se tourner vers de nouveaux publics. Mais un peu d'histoire aidera à comprendre les faits récents, à partir des premières éditions et de celles qui ont suivi. Après avoir été refusé, en 1912, successivement par quatre éditeurs (Fasquelle, Ollendorff, le Mercure de France, et la NRF), Proust publie, à compte d'auteur, chez Grasset, en novembre 1913, la première partie de son roman, intitulée *Du côté de chez Swann*. Le livre est tiré à 3 300 exemplaires. Le volume suivant est mis en préparation chez le même éditeur, mais en août 1914, le déclenchement de la première guerre mondiale interrompt les travaux d'édition. Pendant la guerre Proust, malade et réformé, reprend son projet et l'augmente considérablement. En même temps, il reçoit de Gaston Gallimard, directeur de la maison d'édition de la NRF, qui avait tout d'abord refusé la première partie, la proposition de lui éditer toute la suite à des conditions normales de rémunération. Grasset accepte le départ de Proust et, après la fin des hostilités, la NRF publie à intervalles assez réguliers: en 1919, *A l'ombre des jeunes filles en fleurs* (ainsi qu'une réédition de *Swann* et *Pastiches et Mélanges*); en 1920, *Le Côté de Guermantes I;* en 1921, *Le Côté de Guermantes II* suivi, dans le même volume, de *Sodome et Gomorrhe I;* au printemps 1922, *Sodome et Gomorrhe II,* tandis que Proust meurt le 18 novembre de la même année. Trois parties, achevées, mais en cours de mise au point, restent encore en suspens. La NRF les publie en 1923 pour *La Prisonnière,* en 1925 pour *Albertine disparue,* et en 1927 pour *Le Temps retrouvé.*

Cette première édition, qui a fait connaître Proust, est néanmoins reconnue comme défectueuse. Gallimard la fait reprendre entièrement par deux universitaires, Pierre Clarac et André Ferré, qui mettent au point la nouvelle édition de 1954 dans la Bibliothèque de la Pléiade: pour cela, la nièce et héritière de Proust, Suzy Mante-Proust, les autorise à consulter les manuscrits qu'elle détient. En 1967, le Livre de Poche donne une édition complète avec l'autorisation de Gallimard, et en reprenant exactement le texte de la Pléiade. En 1977, Gallimard à son tour publie une édition de poche dans sa collection Folio, toujours avec le même texte. Les ventes se sont accrues, avec le temps, de façon gigantesque: *Du côté de chez Swann,* toutes éditions confondues, a été vendu, jusqu'en 1987, à 1 500 000 exemplaires, dont 600 000 en Folio; l'ensemble de la *Recherche,* à la même date, toutes parties et toutes éditions confondues, à plus de trois millions d'exemplaires, dont 1,4 million en Folio; la Pléiade, depuis sa parution, à 800 000, au rythme annuel de 6 000 à 8 000. On comprend, par ces chiffres, que

Gallimard ait tout fait pour conserver le monopole qu'il détenait, et que la concurrence ait tenté plusieurs éditeurs.

Les lois sur le domaine littéraire public sont multiples, et certaines, non abolies, remontent jusqu'à la Première République. Sans entrer trop loin dans leur détail, disons que la propriété est protégée en France pendant cinquante ans après la mort de l'écrivain, mais qu'il s'y ajoute des délais supplémentaires si pendant cette période il y a eu une (ou plus d'une) guerre; la loi fixe alors avec précision ces délais, toujours plus grands que la période des hostilités proprement dite. Pour les volumes de Proust parus avant le 24 octobre 1920, la protection est de 50 ans plus 6 ans et 153 jours (première guerre mondiale et après-guerre), plus 8 ans et 122 jours (deuxième guerre mondiale et après-guerre); pour les volumes parus après cette date, elle est de 50 ans plus 8 ans et 122 jours seulement. Les derniers volumes à tomber dans le domaine public, qui étaient en réalité les premiers à avoir été publiés, l'ont fait le 5 octobre 1987. Quant aux posthumes, ils n'ont jamais suscité l'accord entre les juristes, qui s'opposaient des lois contradictoires: l'interprétation la plus favorable à Gallimard les faisait "tomber" en 1985. L'éditeur Flammarion, prêt bien avant cette date à publier une nouvelle édition de *La Prisonnière,* dut donc en demander à Gallimard l'autorisation. Celui-ci recourut alors à une argutie s'appuyant sur le "droit moral," qui appartient aux héritiers de façon "perpétuelle, inaliénable, et imprescriptible" et leur permet de s'opposer à toute entreprise dénaturant l'œuvre: ce qui aurait été le cas, selon Gallimard (se désignant comme l'interprète des héritiers de Proust), si Flammarion commençait son édition générale par *La Prisonnière* et non par *Du côté de chez Swann.* Menacé de procès, ce dernier éditeur préféra traiter, et demanda l'autorisation à Gallimard et à Mme Mante-Proust de publier les trois parties posthumes avant 1987, moyennant le reversement à Mme Mante de 5% du prix de vente de chaque volume; ce qui fut accepté.[1]

Et il est vrai que, depuis quelques années, la date de 1987 avait attiré l'attention de différents éditeurs. Le premier, Flammarion avait songé à une réédition complète dans sa collection de poche G-F et m'avait demandé de constituer à cette fin une équipe de spécialistes. Hachette avait une intention identique avec Le Livre de Poche, mais finit par renoncer. De son côté, Gallimard demanda en 1982 à Jean-Yves Tadié de réunir des collaborateurs pour entreprendre la refonte de la Pléiade. Pour soutenir ce projet qui devait comporter la publication d'une grande quantité de brouillons manuscrits déposés à la Bibliothèque nationale, il signa avec cette dernière, pourtant service public, un contrat qui lui réservait l'exclusivité de publication de ces manuscrits. Plus tard, un autre éditeur, Laffont, se mit en compétition avec sa collection Bouquins, annonçant comme originalité la publication, avec le texte, d'un *Quid* (c'est-à-dire un dictionnaire des curiosités) de Proust.

Ces projets contradictoires, accompagnés d'une certaine agitation publicitaire, ont beaucoup retenu l'attention en 1987. Pourtant, ils ont peut-être masqué aux yeux du public le fait, plus important, que ces nouvelles éditions étaient rendues possibles par les progrès réalisés par les études proustiennes depuis une trentaine d'années. Ces travaux forment aujourd'hui une impressionnante bibliographie. Seulement pour la France, deux périodiques réguliers, le *Bulletin de la Société des Amis de Marcel Proust* et le *Bulletin d'Informations proustiennes,* plus une série de volumes, les *Etudes proustiennes,* éditées par Gallimard, sont consacrés à la production et à l'analyse de ces travaux. De nombreux chercheurs étrangers y participent (y compris Américains et Canadiens), tout en publiant également sur Proust dans leur propre pays. En 1962, puis en 1984, a été acquise par la Bibliothèque nationale la plus grande partie des manuscrits proustiens, offerts désormais à la consultation des spécialistes. La nouvelle publication de la correspondance de Proust, due à l'Américain Philip Kolb, parue jusqu'à l'année 1917, enrichit régulièrement nos connaissances parallèles à l'œuvre. La commémoration du centenaire de Proust en 1971 a donné lieu dans le monde entier à des expositions, colloques, numéros spéciaux et ouvrages de toutes sortes, souvent de grande qualité. C'est en raison de ces activités multiples que l'édition de Clarac et Ferré, après avoir fait autorité pendant trente ans, a paru généralement insuffisante, notamment en ce qui concerne les trois dernières parties. On a constaté que ces érudits n'avaient pas pu examiner certaines dactylographies maintenant retrouvées (*Sodome et Gomorrhe, Albertine disparue*), que certaines "paperoles," collées dans le manuscrit selon un ordre inexact des fragments, n'avaient pas été replacées par eux dans leur continuité pour donner un récit intelligible (la promenade à Versailles dans *La Prisonnière,* par exemple); qu'il y avait parfois eu des erreurs de lecture; que la ponctuation et la disposition typographique voulues par Proust avaient été modifiées dans le sens d'une présentation assez scolaire. Pour les lecteurs modernes, de nombreuses difficultés de compréhension tiennent, dans le détail, à ce que beaucoup d'allusions de l'écrivain sont devenues de moins en moins saisissables à mesure qu'on s'éloigne de son époque, et il est devenu important de les éclaircir dans un apparat de notes. Enfin, l'on peut progressivement dégager, distincte de l'histoire racontée par le récit, une passionnante histoire de la formation et de la composition du roman lui-même, qui en permet une bien meilleure compréhension.

Bien loin d'être une "chute" au sens péjoratif de l'image, l'entrée de la *Recherche* dans le domaine public a en réalité donné lieu à d'importants progrès dans l'édition. Simultanément ont paru, en octobre 1987, l'édition complète de l'œuvre dans la collection G-F, le premier volume de la nouvelle "Pléiade" (*Du côté de chez Swann* et la première moitié d'*A l'ombre des jeunes filles en fleurs*), une édition de luxe d' "Un Amour de Swann" due à Michel Raimond et publiée par l'Imprimerie nationale, une nouvelle *Albertine disparue* chez Grasset et plusieurs ouvrages critiques, tandis que Laffont annonçait pour décembre 1987 son édition complète, sous la direction de Bernard Raffalli, dans sa collection Bouquins.

Pour ce qui regarde l'édition G-F, elle a été l'œuvre d'une équipe homogène, réunie dès 1982, faite de spécialistes universitaires et chercheurs, et comprenant: Bernard Brun pour "Un Amour de Swann" et *Le Temps retrouvé,* Anne Herschberg-Pierrot pour les première et troisième parties de *Du côté de chez Swann,* Danièle Gasiglia-Laster pour les deux volumes d'*A l'ombre des jeunes filles en fleurs,* Elyane Dezon-Jones pour les deux volumes du *Côté de Guermantes,* Emily Eells-Ogée pour les deux volumes de *Sodome et Gomorrhe,* et moi-même pour *La Prisonnière, La Fugitive* et la direction d'ensemble. Les trois volumes posthumes, pour les raisons expliquées précédemment, ont été publiés les premiers (*La Prisonnière* en 1984, *La Fugitive* et *Le Temps retrouvé* en 1986); tous les autres volumes ont été publiés ensemble en 1987. Nous avons voulu que cette édition de poche fût parfaitement maniable, mais offrît en même temps le maximum de garanties scientifiques. Elle s'adresse aussi bien aux amateurs de toujours qu'aux nombreux lecteurs restés sur le seuil de l'univers proustien, hésitant à s'y engager à fond. Cinq années de préparation nous ont été nécessaires. Nous avons collationné les éditions précédentes, les parties données en prépublication dans les revues, et les manuscrits, qu'il s'agît du dernier texte autographe, quand il existe encore, des dactylographies et des épreuves, les unes et les autres souvent surchargées d'additions, ou des nombreux cahiers et feuillets d'ébauches. Nous avons pu suivre la lente et irrégulière maturation du texte, retracer son évolution. Nous avons réparé certaines erreurs de lecture de nos prédécesseurs, adopté dans les derniers volumes (car, pour les précédents, nous avons respecté la présentation telle que Proust l'avait acceptée, si distraitement qu'il l'eût fait) une disposition par paragraphes très longs et avec une ponctuation proche de celle des manuscrits: car de même qu'il se refusait à découper ses longues phrases parce que leur dimension lui paraissait nécessaire, Proust ne voulait pas fragmenter son récit, et n'usait pas fréquemment des alinéas; il ne le faisait guère qu'aux changements d'épisodes; il voulait qu'on reproduisît ses dialogues sans blancs entre les répliques, en intégrant celles-ci dans la continuité du texte; il utilisait beaucoup moins les virgules que ne l'ont fait ses derniers éditeurs; il se conformait à l'usage du débit oral familier ou didactique, qui sépare plus volontiers les groupes de mots dans la phrase par des changements d'intonation que par des pauses; assez souvent même, il insérait des digressions, des apartés, de courtes citations, sans les signaler par aucun signe graphique. Même si nous avons dû parfois rétablir certains de ces signes pour faciliter la compréhension, la présentation que nous avons obtenue est conforme aux intentions déclarées et à la visée esthétique de Proust: celle d'une écriture homogène, intégrant dans une seule coulée les éléments les plus divers, faits décrits, paroles rapportées, niveaux différents de temps et de lieu, dans un immense monologue où doivent être nécessairement rétablies par notre imagination les inflexions de la voix.

Une documentation abondante, conçue comme un auxiliaire de la lecture, accompagne chaque volume. Mais l'encyclopédisme n'est pas dans nos ambitions. Ce qui nous importe est de montrer pour chaque partie du livre les étapes de sa formation, ses particularités thématiques, sa fonction dans l'ensemble, d'aplanir les difficultés de compréhension que ne peut manquer de présenter une œuvre aussi nourrie de culture historique, littéraire et artistique, et aussi liée à une époque maintenant révolue. Nous ne retenons de la biographie que ce qui sert à expliquer l'œuvre: c'est pourquoi nous évoquons succinctement la rencontre de Proust avec Alfred Agostinelli, leur cohabitation, la fuite d'Alfred, les démarches pour le ramener et sa mort, ces éléments entrant largement dans la composition du personnage d'Albertine. Nous publions des lettres dans lesquelles l'écrivain précise ses projets, raconte par avance telle partie du roman, prend position sur les clés qu'on donne pour ses personnages, cherche à se renseigner sur des points précis (comme les robes de Fortuny), ou encore débat avec l'éditeur de la publication en cours. Nous reproduisons certains articles, comme celui qui double l'épisode de Venise, tel qu'il a paru dans *Feuillets d'art* sous une forme différente de l'édition. Notre système de notes, fort simple, éclaire les allusions, fournit les explications génétiques, propose l'interprétation des passages difficiles, justifie les corrections les plus importantes. Des dossiers sur l'accueil des volumes successifs par la critique permettent de suivre la carrière de l'œuvre auprès des journalistes, et de mesurer sur documents combien il a fallu de temps pour que se généralise une compréhension fondée sur autre chose que le pittoresque social ou le scandale. Tout cet appareil n'a en vue que de proposer aux lecteurs la possibilité d'une lecture compétente, de stimuler leur intérêt; il ne veut en aucun cas faire écran à leur plaisir.

Alors que notre édition de *La Fugitive* avait paru l'année précédente, une nouvelle et différente a été présentée en 1987 par Nathalie Mauriac et Etienne Wolff, chez Grasset. Son texte est établi sur une ultime dactylographie revue par Proust dans les derniers jours de sa vie, totalement inconnue jusqu'ici et retrouvée récemment dans la succession de Mme Mante-Proust. Le titre retenu en définitive par l'écrivain est *Albertine disparue,* que nous mêmes avions eu la prudence de garder en sous-titre en attendant que d'éventuels éclaircissements jaillissent un jour. L'essentiel de cette nouvelle édition semble résider dans le sacrifice de 250 pages de la première version, remplacées par une brève addition difficilement raccordée au reste. Nous y apprenons qu'Albertine est morte d'un accident de cheval à Combray, et non en Touraine; le héros en déduit qu'elle s'y était rendue pour retrouver Mlle Vinteuil et son amie, et qu'il est donc bien certain qu'elle était homosexuelle. Les multiples recherches, sans résultats définitifs, qu'il organisait pour savoir quelle avait été sa vie secrète, sont devenues inutiles. Cela expliquerait l'importante suppression. Une fois de plus se manifeste l'état d'inachèvement réel des derniers volumes, dont le remaniement continuait bien après que Proust eût écrit le mot "fin," laissant subsister pour nous des incertitudes. L'écrivain n'aurait-il pas, *in extremis,* donné l'instruction de ne pas tenir compte de ces ultimes corrections, ce qui expliquerait pourquoi son frère Robert les a négligées en éditant le volume? S'il a vraiment eu l'intention de faire cette vaste coupure, n'aurait-il pas, s'il avait vécu plus longtemps, repris cet abondant matériau, tout rédigé et admirable à ses propres yeux (comme l'attestent plusieurs passages de ses lettres)? On sait qu'il laissait rarement perdre les passages supprimés et qu'il les reprenait dans d'autres parties. Mais comment utiliser ces 250 pages dans *Le Temps retrouvé,* déjà engorgé, si *Albertine disparue* se réduit à un court épisode servant d'appendice à *La Prisonnière?* La trouvaille de Nathalie Mauriac pose plus de problèmes qu'elle n'en résout, et son édition n'invalide nullement la nôtre, mais incite au contraire à comparer les deux fins de l'histoire d'Albertine, en continuant d'attendre que d'autres découvertes nous apportent des clartés—ou des énigmes—nouvelles.

Que dire un an après le début de cette effervescence sur les rééditions? D'abord, qu'elle n'a pas été un feu de paille médiatique suivi d'épaisses ténèbres. Les divers volumes présentés au public se vendent, et même bien. G-F en est à une seconde édition, revue et mise à jour. "Bouquins" s'occupe de faire corriger un "Quid" dont les erreurs étaient trop évidentes. La Pléiade va publier son troisième volume. "Folio" est en cours de refonte, sur le modèle de G-F. Certes, les lecteurs ont encore à surmonter leur perplexité devant les offres multiples, mais peu à peu une répartition des choix s'opère en fonction des besoins d'information, de la maniabilité des volumes, de leur lisibilité, de leur prix. Tous semblent conscients que ces éditions nouvelles constituent un progrès. Les différences leur garantissent une liberté de bon aloi, en les obligeant à une réflexion préalable. Après les tout premiers articles de presse, souvent et inévitablement hâtifs, viennent maintenant des études patientes et approfondies, comme le remarquable article de Roger Shattuck et Douglas Alden, "Searching for the True Text," paru dans le *Times Literary Supplement* du 10 au 16 juin 1988.

Le vaste écho que Proust trouve à l'étranger se manifeste par des traductions nouvelles ou des refontes de traductions anciennes. La Chine, qui ignorait cet écrivain jusqu'à une époque très récente, voit plusieurs équipes entreprendre sa traduction. L'Italie a une nouvelle traduction en cours. Le Japon se prépare à faire de même. Les Etats-Unis attendent la traduction entièrement nouvelle (et faite d'après le texte de G-F) que Richard Howard prépare pour Farrar Straus Giroux. Enfin—last but not least—la série de manifestations, d'expositions, de cours et de conférences organisées par l'Université d'Alabama à Birmingham à l'occasion du 75ème anniversaire de la publication de *Swann* est une brillante démonstration de la pérennité et même de l'extension des études proustiennes.

Les nouvelles éditions, dans leur grand nombre et leur variété, sont à la fois une conséquence de la très grande richesse d'un écrivain par rapport auquel s'ordonnent tous ceux de notre siècle, et un signe quantitatif et qualitatif de la vitalité de la recherche universitaire proustienne en France.

Note

[1]Voir à ce sujet l'article de Claude Rivière, "Proust écrivain public," dans *Le Journal littéraire* d'octobre 1987.

8

Shakespeare and Proust

Philip Kolb

THE FIRST PERSON TO HAVE associated Proust with Shakespeare
was Charles Scott Moncrieff, who translated Proust's novel into English.
His solution to the problem of the work's general title, *A la recherche du
temps perdu,* was to borrow a line from Shakespeare's thirtieth sonnet:

> When to the sessions of sweet silent thought
> I summon up remembrance of things past.

Admittedly, *Remembrance of Things Past* is a title that has a poetic
resonance. It falls short of the particular purpose of the title, however,
because it fails to include its key word, which is Time, the novel's principal
theme. Proust was distressed to learn how his title had been translated.
The first to solve that problem was James Grieve of the Australian National
University, who, for his new translation of *Du côté de chez Swann,* chose
to entitle the entire work *A Search for Lost Time.* Grieve placed the word
Time at the beginning of the first sentence of the first volume. In doing
so, he found an ingenious way of following Proust's own inspiration.
The author had wanted to indicate his principal theme by placing the word
Time at the beginning of the first sentence, as well as at the end of the last
sentence of the entire work. Grieve translates the first sentence in these
words: "Time was when I always went to bed early."[1] That was a
masterstroke.

The first person to join the names of Shakespeare and Proust in a
meaningful way was Etienne Brunet, to whom we owe a concordance of
Proust's novel. In his introduction, Brunet speaks of the "great texts like

the Bible, the Summa of Saint Thomas, the work of Shakespeare or that of
Proust" as being more readily available to the computer than those of lesser
authors.[2] As we can see, he places Proust in good company.

Proust's name was again ranked alongside that of Shakespeare not
long ago, when several European literary magazines took a referendum
among their readers to inquire whom they considered to be the greatest writers of their respective countries. After Shakespeare, Goethe, Cervantes,
Dante, and Kafka, the author who, in this literary game, was classified as
the foremost of all French writers, even surpassing Molière, Voltaire,
Balzac, and all the others, was Marcel Proust.[3] Proust's standing was further consolidated when, in October 1987, the copyright expired on his
novel. That event was marked by the publication of three new editions of
his work, all of them annotated, their text established by teams of scholars
from the original manuscripts, notebooks, proof sheets, and other documents. Of these new publications, the most complete and authoritative is
the Pléiade edition, whose general editor is Jean-Yves Tadié, a professor of
French literature at the Sorbonne and France's foremost Proust scholar. In
a brilliant general introduction to the first volume of his edition, Tadié tells
how Proust took as his models, not one of his successful contemporaries,
whose fame has since faded into oblivion, but such writers as Balzac, Saint-
Simon, Baudelaire, whose renown increased after their death. Moreover,
Tadié describes the extraordinary method of work that Proust adopted: how
he would reject, revise, begin anew, improving, adding, arranging, rear-
ranging, assembling, reassembling pages, episodes, characters, working
tirelessly and persistently, always striving to improve what he had already
written, in order to reach ever and ever nearer his ideal. That, says Tadié, is
how a writer creates a work that goes beyond its period, beyond its country
or its author, and whose fame never ceases to increase. For years, it has
been said that, in that category of writers, England had its Shakespeare,
Germany its Goethe, Italy its Dante, but France seemed not to have one
whose stature dominated that of all the others sufficiently to belong to that
supreme class. But now, finally, judging by the vast number of studies that
have been devoted to Marcel Proust, to every aspect of his work, it would
appear that France has at long last, today,—and that she will have in the
future,—as the greatest of all those of her rich heritage, counting so many
centuries of illustrious writers, *her* Proust.[4]

This claim that Proust can be considered the peer of Shakespeare
may cause some to demur, asking whether it can be fully justified. So I

would like to examine this question and consider briefly what, if anything, Proust has in common with England's great playwright.

One of the principal traits of Shakespeare's genius, it seems to me, is his consummate mastery of the English language. His vocabulary is stupendous; where a peasant in Shakespeare's time would use about five hundred words, a man who had studied at a university, some three to four thousand, Milton, seven thousand, Thackeray five thousand, Shakespeare, as we know from studies of his works, had a vocabulary that has been calculated to come to some twenty thousand words.[5] Besides, he knew Latin, Italian, Spanish, and had a sufficient command of French to pun in it. There is evidence in his plays indicating that he was conversant with the language of heraldry, hunting, fencing, military tactics, equitation, legal terminology. Our English of today borrows as is generally known, from a myriad of Shakespeare's pungent expressions. He had ways of expressing himself that are breathtaking in their beauty. Consider how, to tell his audience that night is ending and day dawning, he conveys this simple concept:

> Night's candles are burnt out, and jocund day
> Stands tiptoe on the misty mountain tops.[6]

Here is his whimsical way of speaking of love:

> Tell me where is fancy bred,
> Or in the heart or in the head?
> How begot, how nourished?
>   Reply, reply.
> It is engendered in the eyes
> With gazing fed; and fancy dies
> In the cradle where it lies.[7]

Proust, too, had an inspired gift for metaphor and for poetic expression. All things considered, much of what we said earlier of Shakespeare can, in my opinion, and allowing for the difference in their cultural heritage, be said of Proust. He had an encyclopaedic fund of knowledge, was especially interested in literature, history, philosophy, botany, medicine; he read widely in many fields, taking a keen interest in the world around him, whether it was in the social or the political sphere or in the sciences. He was indeed steeped in the literary and artistic culture of the western world. He knew by heart much of Racine, most of the French poets of the nineteenth century, and was familiar with novelists of France, England, and Russia. To read Proust with full comprehension, we need some acquaintance with Gothic architecture, with painting of the Italian Renaissance, with the Dutch masters of the seventeenth century, with French painters of the nineteenth and early twentieth centuries. Similarly, we might miss numerous hidden allusions to Balzac's novels, and to the literature of many other authors of France of the seventeenth and nineteenth centuries, if we were unfamiliar with the works of those writers.

Consequently, Proust's scope is vast, his vocabulary extremely rich and varied. Brunet's study of that subject, which I mentioned earlier, counts more than eighteen thousand words.[8] That figure is particularly impressive when we consider the fact that most French writers are more conservative than English and American ones, and that Proust takes few liberties with his language, seldom using neologisms. A Canadian scholar, Victor Graham, has done a study of imagery in Proust's work.[9] Graham shows Proust's metaphors to be enriched by a fund of knowledge in various sciences, such as medicine, astronomy, archeology, geology. Proust's virtuosity in dealing with imagery, as well as matters of syntax, description, and so forth, bears the unmistakable stamp of genius. All aspects of his style have, in fact, been scrupulously studied by scholars, whose findings seem to justify the wide interest and admiration that his work has elicited. Specialists in numerous fields have examined in detail his various techniques. With Proust, as with Shakespeare, one would like to quote, and quote endlessly, but our space here is not unlimited.

Perhaps it is this depth, this rich texture of his novel, and, in particular, the length and complexity of some of Proust's sentences, that have discouraged many readers on their first perusal of his prose. A few samples of his manner may instill confidence in prospective readers, encouraging them to venture farther into his novel. Since we have quoted the lovely verse in which Shakespeare announces the dawn, let us see how Proust manages to call forth a visual image of some lilacs in a modest country garden:

> [. . .] in the open air, [. . .] dangling here and there among the foliage, light and pliant in their fresh mauve frocks, clusters of young lilacs swayed in the breeze without heeding the passer-by [. . .]. I recognised in them the purple-clad platoons posted at the entrance to M. Swann's

park in the warm spring afternoons, like an enchanting rustic tapestry.
[. . .] A cold wind swept through it, as at Combray, but in the middle
of this rich, moist, rural land, which might have been on the banks of
the Vivonne, there had nevertheless arisen, punctual at the trysting
place like all its band of brothers, a great white pear-tree which waved
smilingly in the sun's face, like a curtain of light materialised and made
palpable, its flowers shaken by the breeze but polished and glazed with
silver by the sun's rays.[10]

Notice how the lilacs here are linked with the ones described in the chapter
on Combray. Note, too, how Proust structures his novel through such
passages, which echo one another by means of linked metaphors, recurrent
themes, and other such devices.

Another reason for our admiration of Shakespeare is his way of
revealing personality traits by his use of dialogue. Although he presents
most of his characters as being entirely good or evil, we can recognize a
certain psychological depth in some of his creations (Lear, or Hotspur, for
instance). Proust, too, uses dialogue to great effect in his novel in order to
show, through a character's manner of expression, what are that person's
origins or social status, or mental processes. The notion that Proust is
wordy is baseless; it has been suggested perhaps by some who have read
him superficially. Let me give an example that shows how simply and
succinctly he tells us of the narrator's relationship with his father: "The
contempt which my father had for my kind of intelligence was so far
tempered by affection that, in practice, his attitude towards everything I did
was one of blind indulgence."[11] Here, in a single sentence, he has given
the reader an insight into a rather complex relationship. Instead of wordi-
ness, what we find in Proust, on the contrary, is an amazing density and, of
course, a psychological depth that is unsurpassed in literature of any
period.

Yet another feature of Shakespeare's works that we hold in high
esteem is their poetic tonality. In *A Midsummer Night's Dream,* Lysander
tells Helena that he is going to meet Hermia at midnight; he designates the
hour in this effervescent display of imagery:

> . . . when Phoebe doth behold
> Her silver visage in the wat'ry glass
> Decking with liquid pearl the bladed grass. . .[12]

Proust's work is similarly fused with poetry, especially in his evocations of nature, as was exemplified by the lilac description, and generally in his view of the universe. In this last respect, he belongs to the great tradition of French writers, the so-called *moralistes,* like Montaigne, Pascal, La Rochefoucauld, La Bruyère, who express their thoughts reflecting on manners, mores, human nature. In the course of his narrative, Proust pauses now and then to comment on whatever he has been discussing, usually making a passing remark in the form of a maxim or an aphorism. His work is punctuated by a rich fund of these remarks that express some of his views on life in general. Here, for instance, is one of these maxims: "To make reality endurable we are all obliged to encourage in ourselves a few small foibles."[13] Then we have this gently ironic observation about our penchant toward self-delusion: "[. . .] to each one of us clear ideas are those which have the same degree of confusion as our own."[14] Here is another one concerning egocentrism: "Man is the creature who cannot get outside of himself, who knows others only in himself, and, when he says the contrary, lies."[15] This is what the author thinks of our ability to understand our fellowmen, along with an astute comment about scientific knowledge: "The unknown element in other people's lives is like the unknown element in nature, which every scientific discovery merely reduces but does not suppress."[16] What an apt commentary Proust makes here on theories of the origin of the universe, each one of which seems to contradict the one that preceded it! And this aphorism, concerning theory versus experimentation: "Every activity of the mind is easy if it need not take reality into account."[17] Here is one that has a slightly Shakespearean, or Pascalean, tinge to it: "The mind has its own fleeting landscapes."[18] Or this one about our subjective view of our surroundings: "The universe is true for all of us and different for each of us."[19] And one last example, concerning relativity and our penchant toward self-delusion: "A cathedral, a wave in a storm, a dancer's leap, never turns out to be as high as we had hoped [. . .].[20]

Shakespeare's plays abound in humor, although most of it is of the rollicking sort intended to amuse and hold the attention of the common folk in his audience. Here is a sample:

FALSTAFF.   I will not lend thee a penny.
PISTOL.   Why, then the world's my oyster,
                      Which I with sword will open.[21]

Proust's novel, too, is suffused with humor, but most of it is in a more gentle, subtle vein. Unfortunately, we cannot quote at sufficient length to do it justice. Here is a sample in a brief excerpt taken from the conversation at the dinner to which the narrator's family invites Swann; the grandfather is speaking:

> "[. . .] Hullo! you two; you never thanked him for the Asti," he went on, turning to his sisters-in-law.
>
> "What! we never thanked him? I think, between you and me, that I put it to him quite neatly," replied my aunt Flora.
>
> "Yes, you managed it very well; I admired you for it," said my aunt Céline.
>
> "But you did it very prettily, too."
>
> "Yes; I was rather proud of my remark about 'nice neighbors.' "
>
> "What! Do you call that thanking him?" shouted my grandfather. "I heard that all right, but devil take me if I guessed it was meant for Swann. You may be quite sure he never noticed it."
>
> "Come, come; Swann isn't a fool. I'm sure he understood. You didn't expect me to tell him the number of bottles, or to guess what he paid for them."[22]

What separates these two great creators, besides the chasm of some three hundred years intervening between the periods in which they lived, is the fact that Shakespeare, as a man of the theatre, had to concern himself with pleasing his audience, just as Molière would do in the following century. Proust, on the other hand, being a novelist, had principally to earn the appreciation of his eventual readers. One of his main preoccupations was to perfect the structure, the architecture of his great edifice. He knew how we tend to admire the anonymous sculptures of the great cathedrals of Chartres or Amiens, even when they may be hidden from view (Ruskin, whom Proust had translated, had explored them in depth); so he could hope that some of his readers would have sufficient discernment to come to perceive the hidden elements of his novel's structure, and to admire the beauties of its intricately intertwined themes. It would have given him great satisfaction had he known how many scholars in every civilized country of the world would devote years of intent study exploring his novel in its structure and in its many other facets.

Here is how Proust calls forth a visual image of a ballet dancer whom the narrator notices when he goes behind the scenes of a theatre; it ends on a striking example of his use of metaphor (unfortunately diminished in translation); it also shows his virtuosity in the handling of syntax:

> I was delighted to observe, in the thick of a crowd of journalists or men of fashion, admirers of the actresses, who were greeting one another, talking, smoking, as though at a party in town, a young man in a black velvet cap and hortensia-colored skirt, his cheeks chalked in red like a page from a Watteau album, who with smiling lips and eyes raised to the ceiling, describing graceful patterns with the palms of his hands and springing lightly into the air, seemed so entirely of another species from the sensible people in everyday clothes in the midst of whom he was pursuing like a madman the course of his ecstatic dream, so alien to the preoccupations of their life, so anterior to the habits of their civilisation, so enfranchised from the laws of nature, that it was as restful and refreshing a spectacle as watching a butterfly straying through a crowd to follow with one's eyes, between the flats, the natural arabesques traced by his winged, capricious, painted curvetings.[23]

As I have said, we cannot in any absolute sense compare writers of such vastly different periods in the history of literature. But there is much in the work of each of them that partakes of life and evinces a profound understanding of humanity. I would like to share with you an excerpt from one of my favorite passages in Proust's work, a consultation that the narrator's grandmother has with Dr. du Boulbon. The physician is telling her about a man he saw in a home for neurasthenics, suggesting that she should not be offended if he compares her to him, because he considers that man to be the greatest poet of his time.

> That poor lunatic is the most lofty intellect that I know. Submit to being called a neurotic. You belong to that splendid and pitiable family which is the salt of the earth. Everything we think of as great has come to us from neurotics. It is they and they alone who found religions and create great works of art. The world will never realise how much it owes to them, and what they have suffered in order to bestow their gifts on it. We enjoy fine music, beautiful paintings, a thousand exquisite things, but we do not know what they cost those who

wrought them in insomnia, tears, spasmodic laughter, urticaria, asthma, epilepsy, a terror of death which is worse than any of these [. . .][24]

The mention of asthma seems to be inserted here as a sort of discreet signature of the author; it reminds us of the butterfly with which Whistler signed his paintings.

And here, finally, is an example to show what power and what brevity Proust can display in a poignant scene. This dramatic episode occurs in the hotel dining room in Venice, during the narrator's sojourn with his mother in that city:

> A waiter came to tell me that my mother was expecting me. I went to join her and made my apologies to Mme Sazerat, saying that I had been amused to see Mme de Villeparisis. At the sound of this name, Mme Sazerat turned pale and seemed about to faint. Controlling herself with an effort: "Mme de Villeparisis who was Mlle de Bouillon?" she inquired.
>
> "Yes."
>
> "Couldn't I just get a glimpse of her for a moment? It has been the dream of my life."
>
> "Then there's no time to lose, Madame, for she will soon have finished her dinner. But how do you come to take such an interest in her?"
>
> "Because Mme de Villeparisis was, before her second marriage, the Duchesse d'Havré, beautiful as an angel, wicked as a demon, who drove my father to distraction, ruined him and then abandoned him immediately. Well, she may have behaved toward him like the lowest prostitute, she may have been the cause of our having had to live, my family and myself, in humble circumstances at Combray, but now that my father is dead, my consolation is to think that he loved the most beautiful woman of his generation, and as I've never set eyes on her, it will be a sort of solace in spite of everything. . ."
>
> I escorted Mme Sazerat, trembling with emotion, to the restaurant and pointed out Mme de Villeparisis.
>
> But, like a blind person who looks everywhere but in the right direction, Mme Sazerat could not bring her eyes to rest upon the table at which Mme de Villeparisis was dining, but, looking towards another part of the room, said:
>
> "But she must have gone, I don't see her where you say she is."

> And she continued to gaze round the room in quest of the loathed, adored vision that had haunted her imagination for so long.
>
> "Yes, there she is, at the second table."
>
> "Then we can't be counting from the same point. At what I count as the second table there's only an old gentleman and a little hunchbacked, red-faced hideous woman."
>
> "That's she!"[25]

This example shows how mistaken it would be to suppose that Proust is necessarily wordy or long-winded, and that nothing happens in his novel. Of course, the scale of his fresco is vast, but it does present many moments of surprise or dramatic suspense. Some readers may be unaware of this feature of his work. For their information, here is my count of these unexpected reversals: there are 146 of them in Proust's novel.

Perhaps, as we have indicated, it may not be quite valid to compare a man of genius writing in the late sixteenth century with one who composed his work early in the twentieth. We do not even know, in point of fact, just who did write the works attributed to William Shakespeare; whether they were composed by the actor known by that name, whose existence is vouchsafed for in records showing that he lived and died at Stratford-on-Avon, a man who had little schooling but a keen mind for business dealings, whose daughters could neither read nor write, and whose last will and testament listed no library, not even a single book; or else, by that other William, William Stanley, sixth Earl of Derby, who was a student at Oxford, who then travelled with his tutor on the continent, and who is known to have been a man of considerable culture, and who was possessed of a passion for writing plays. This question, as is generally known, was debated not long ago before two justices of the Supreme Court of the United States, although they declined to render a decision by naming the true author of the plays. If the author of the work attributed to Shakespeare was indeed the sixth Earl of Derby, that would give us one more link between Shakespeare and Proust, because we know that a descendant of William Stanley, the seventeenth Lord Derby, met and dined with Marcel Proust in December, 1918.[26] Whether or not we know the identity of the author, we are fortunate enough to have the works attributed to Shakespeare as they have come down to us in the folios, whoever their author may have been. Their existence suffices to enrich us abundantly, as does the work of Marcel Proust.

Now, if I may end on a personal note, I would like to tell what it means to me to see Proust's name juxtaposed with that of Shakespeare. When I arrived in Paris for the first time as a student in 1935 and told people that the subject of my Ph.D. thesis was Proust's correspondence, they eyed me askance, as if I had come from another planet. Not many in those days were convinced that Proust was truly as great a writer as I considered him to be. Their attitude was doubtless conditioned by a world-wide depression, and by fears—only too well founded—of a second world war. People at that time were inclined to look on pure literature as something of a luxury. Few of them dreamed that Proust would some day be considered one of France's greatest writers, ranked alongside of Shakespeare. But time has passed, and I have witnessed a change in the attitude of the reading public toward Proust's work that is, in some respects, similar to the change he describes in the nineteenth-century public's attitude toward Renoir's paintings.[27] To me, Proust's ascension in world literature, as it has evolved over the past half century, seems to justify the years I spent investigating his letters, his life, and his works. It gives me great satisfaction to know that his genius is finally viewed, the world over, in its proper perspective. We can see evidence of that recognition in the splendid commemoration of the seventy-fifth anniversary of the first volume of Proust's novel, which Professor William Carter and his colleagues have so admirably organized at the University of Alabama at Birmingham, an event that will long be remembered as a consecration of Proust's place in literary history.

Notes

[1]In *The New York Times Magazine*, September 25, 1988, pp. 42 and 44, Richard Howard announces, with a flourish, his intention to do a new translation of Proust's novel on the basis of the Garnier-Flammarion edition of 1987. He gives his version of the first paragraph of the first volume, imitating Grieve's *trouvaille*. In an attempt to justify his borrowing from Grieve, he criticizes the latter's adding the word "always." A rendering that would improve over both Grieve's and Howard's would be: "Time was when I used to go to bed early" (thus combining Grieve's beginning with the more fitting verb tense of Scott Moncrieff-Kilmartin).

[2]Etienne Brunet, *Le Vocabulaire de Marcel Proust* I. Etude quantitative. Genève-Paris: Slatkine, 1983, p. 1.

[3]Pierre Assouline et François Taillandier, "Enquête," in *Lire*, no. 145 (octobre 1987), p. 43.

[4]Marcel Proust, *A la recherche du temps perdu*, I, édition publiée sous la direction de Jean-Yves Tadié. Paris: Gallimard, 1987, pp. x-xi.

[5]G. L. Brook, *The Language of Shakespeare*, London: Deutsch, 1976, chapter 2, p. 26. Cf. Jacques Boulenger, *L'affaire Shakespeare*. Paris: Simon Kra, 1919, p. 11.

[6]*Romeo and Juliet*, III, 5, lines 9-10.

[7]*The Merchant of Venice*, III, ii, lines 63-69.

[8]Brunet, vol. I, p. ii.

[9]Victor E. Graham, *The Imagery of Proust*, Oxford: Blackwell, 1966.

[10]Marcel Proust, *A la recherche du temps perdu, Le Côté de Guermantes*, vol. 2, p. 157; *Guermantes Way*, Kilmartin, vol. II, p. 157.

[11]Ibid., vol. I, *A l'ombre des jeunes filles en fleurs*, p. 45; vol. I, *Within a Budding Grove*, p. 490.

[12]*A Midsummer Night's Dream*, I, i, lines 209-11.

[13]*The Maxims of Marcel Proust*, edited, with a translation by Justin O'Brien, New York: Columbia University Press, 1948, maxim no. 2. *A l'ombre des jeunes filles en fleurs*, I, 591; Kilmartin, *Within a Budding Grove*, I, 636.

[14]O'Brien, no. 35. *A l'ombre des jeunes filles en fleurs*, I, 552; Kilmartin, I, 594.

[15]O'Brien, no. 47. *La Fugitive*, III, 450; Kilmartin, III, 459.

[16]O'Brien, no. 53. *La Prisonnière*, 392; Kilmartin III, 398.

[17]O'Brien, no. 58. *Sodome et Gomorrhe*, II, 650; Kilmartin, II, 674.

[18]O'Brien, no. 63. *Le Temps retrouvé*, III, 1035; Kilmartin, III, 1092.

[19]O'Brien, no. 68. *La Prisonnière*, III, 191; Kilmartin, III, 189.

[20]O'Brien, no. 379. *A l'ombre des jeunes filles en fleurs*, I, 528; Kilmartin, I, 568.

[21]*The Merry Wives of Windsor*, II, ii, 2-4.

[22]*Du côté de chez Swann*, I, 34-35; Kilmartin, I, 37.

[23]*Le Côté de Guermantes*, II, 177; *The Guermantes Way*, vol. II, p. 180.

[24]*Le Côté de Guermantes*, II, 305; *The Guermantes Way*, vol. II, p. 315.

[25]*La Fugitive*, III, 633-34; *The Fugitive*, vol. III, pp. 648-49.

[26]*New York Times*, Saturday, 26 September 1987, I, 1:1, "You-know-who Wrote the Plays, Judges say," by Irving Molotsky.

[27]*Le Côté de Guermantes*, II, 327; *The Guermantes Way*, vol. II, p. 338.

9

Swann Is Seventy-five Years Old

Wallace Fowlie

I BELIEVE I AM HERE, IN THIS SPOT, at this moment, about to speak to you of Swann, because of longevity, of time. I claim to being a reader of Proust longer than anyone in my audience this evening. I read *Un Amour de Swann* at nineteen, just a few years after Proust had died. By twenty I had finished reading *A la recherche* in the old sixteen-volume edition of Gallimard. I am still reading it, now in the Pléiade edition, and still marvelling at how much I discover in it at each new reading.

When Professor Carter, in November 1986, assigned to me the topic of this talk: *Swann Is Seventy-five Years Old,* I felt honored. In my letter of acceptance, I pointed out that if I reached November 1988, I would be eighty, five years older than Swann, and thus perhaps a worthier candidate for canonization.

Let me say that the name of Swann has haunted me ever since I received that invitation in 1986 to participate in this symposium. Through all those months I often chided myself by saying: "Stop worrying. After all, Swann is not that big a subject. Swann is not all of Proust's novel, neither the character Charles Swann, nor that first volume, *Du côté de chez Swann*." The chiding did little good, because as possible thoughts and plots for my lecture began to form in my mind and in my memory, I realized that, indeed, Swann is all of Proust's novel. His presence is in all of those aspects of the novel we study and cherish, and which we name in turn "psychological," "sociological," "aesthetic." But uppermost in our remembrance of *A la recherche,* is Swann in his human relationships with so many of the characters, especially of course with Marcel. He is a friend, and often a close friend of many of the Guermantes. Swann knows and admires the three characters who represent accomplishments in creative work: Bergotte the novelist-friend of his daughter; Elstir the painter whom we knew first as M. Biche in the Verdurin coterie, and the composer Vinteuil, whose sonata makes real to him his love for Odette.

Yes, Swann is more pervasive, more present in the novel than any other character save Marcel in his dual role of narrator and protagonist. The reasons seem to be two-fold. There is a great deal of Marcel Proust in Swann, and Marcel in the novel seems to derive from Swann who guides the boy and the man in his tastes, his intuitions, his actions, in his capacity for love, and in his very special understanding of love. It would not be too hazardous to propose the thesis that Swann and Marcel in an essential way form one character.

We are introduced to Swann early in *Swann's Way,* and his appearance is associated in the mind of the boy with a sound. The family is on vacation in Combray where they stay in Tante Léonie's house. After dinner they usually spend some time in the garden. The ringing of the garden gate bell announces the arrival of their neighbor M. Swann, who comes at that time to join them. This event is described as a frequent occurrence. But soon after that opening passage, the ringing of that bell is described late one special evening when Swann has been dining with the family, and the boy Marcel is in his room upstairs, anguished over not having his usual good night kiss from his mother. He hears the bell and knows it means Swann has left and soon he may have the chance to have that kiss.

Three thousand pages later in the novel, on the very last page, Marcel, a middle-aged man attending a social reception of the Guermantes in their new house, hears the sound of that bell, *le tintement de la clochette.* His memory becomes audible after he has met and talked with many of the friends he has known throughout his life. His oldest and greatest friend was Swann, who has died. That evening he had talked with Swann's wife (now Mme de Forcheville), with Swann's daughter (now la marquise de Saint-Loup), and with Swann's granddaughter, Mlle de Saint-Loup.

The sound of the garden gate bell of Combray so many years later in the grandest of all social events of the novel, was the memory of Swann. *Le tintement de la clochette* is not merely an echo Proust speaks of on his last page. It is a gracious recall of Swann, the most gracious of all the Proustian characters. It is one of the most deeply felt sentimental mourning moments in the novel for the reader. Chronological time is uppermost in our usual reading of those last pages of the book. But the sound of the bell

Marcel hears is triumph over the passing of time. It is the last instance we have of involuntary memory.

The manner of Proust's writing makes it difficult for us to see a unified picture of any of the major characters. We often have the impression of seeing just a silhouette of the duchess, or a series of fugitive poses of Charlus. Each one is fused with a milieu—Norpois, for example, or Françoise—and each one remains close to the impressions and sentiments of Marcel, whether it be Albertine or Morel. In our hope to see a unified picture of a given character, we forget that Proust was writing a novel and a memoir book. Memoirs are often a series of anecdotes.

Swann is a living character both before his death and after his death. At his first appearance in Combray, three descriptive details are given which are often repeated later: *nez busqué, yeux verts, cheveux presque roux.* It is little to go on, but perhaps it is enough: the arch of his nose, the green of his eyes, the ruddiness of his hair. There is only one detail on his closeness to Marcel's family: Swann's father, a stockbroker, had been a friend of Marcel's grandfather.

More than one critic has pointed out the three poles or three centers around which Proust constructs his novel: love, society, and art. When we read the second chapter of *Swann's Way: Un Amour de Swann,* we realize that single chapter, a strong chapter, almost isolated by itself, exemplifies the theory. There Swann appears in his triple function of lover, man of the world, and amateur (or lover of the arts). Proust uses Swann for his first study of passion, the basis of all subsequent studies of passion in *A la recherche.* As we watch Swann in the Verdurin clan, Proust gives us an image of a Paris world and of Swann as a connoisseur of Italian painting and of the Dutch painter Vermeer about whom he intends to write a study.

In the first chapter, *Combray,* Swann is a mysterious figure for Marcel's family. Amiable and courteous, elegantly dressed, Swann is appreciated by them as a friendly neighbor, but they have no understanding of his high social situation. He is among the first people outside of his family to whom Marcel is attracted and whom he admires. Swann talks to him, gives him copies of Italian paintings, and tells him about Bergotte. Marcel's avidity to learn is nurtured by Swann who leads the boy away from family conversations to those about art and ideas.

The term "psychic pluralism" explains a trait of Proustian characters: the multiple traits in a man's character which often contradict one another, and which surprise and puzzle the reader and other characters in the novel.

Swann and Charlus are leading examples of psychic pluralism. We know Swann first as the son of a Jewish stockbroker, member of the Jockey Club, a friend of the Prince of Wales. And yet this friendly neighbor is considered by Marcel's family a *déclassé*. He has married Odette, a courtesan as she is called. She is not invited with her husband to the dinner at Combray.

After his frenzied and jealous love for Odette comes to an end, he marries her and thus possibly endangers his social life. Most of his friends continue to see him even if some of them ostracize Odette. We continue to think of him throughout the work as lover, socialite, and art connoisseur, and, because of fidelity to his race, as defender of Dreyfus. Even that stand did not very much affect his social life. It turned him back to the origins of his race, visible at the end of his life in the modifications of his face. He knew the disease that was to take his life was fatal, and he was resigned, in a noble way, to death.

Less than a character, Swann is best characterized as a witness, a presence in the book. He is not given the powerful relief that Proust gives to Charlus in that man's actions and behavior. Swann is a quieter personage, a more finely drawn representative of his historical moment and milieu than Charlus is.

Reserved and dignified, yes, but a man who throughout the first half of the novel, is quietly revealing the experiences of his life to Marcel, and thus providing the future novelist with the subject matter of his book. I have now come to my sermon text. We are again at the end of the work, on the last page of *Le Temps retrouvé* where the name of Swann is evoked more deliberately and explicitly than in any other part of the novel.

The reception scene is in a way a review of all of Marcel's life. He has just received the revelation that will force him to write his book. He is convinced, in an almost abrupt way, that his book is in him. This leads him to a second realization. He says, "The subject matter of my experience, the subject matter of my book, came to me from Swann (*la matière de mon livre me venait de Swann*).

We are at the end of the matinée scene of *Le Temps retrouvé,* which is the end of the novel. Marcel has just seen coming toward him, at the side of Gilberte, a girl of sixteen. "Time," he says to himself, "had materialized itself in this girl." And then he names her: "Mlle de Saint-Loup was standing in front of me." Her nose, in the form of a beak and curved, was not like that of Swann, but like Saint-Loup's. Marcel ends his description of her by saying that this girl, Swann's granddaughter, was like his own youth.

Then, in a striking analogy, unexpected at this point, but allowing Proust to reconstruct his novel, he compares the book to a culinary creation of Françoise, that *bœuf à la gelée* which M. de Norpois had found so delicious. He makes then a statement, crucial for our understanding of Proust's art. "Impressions derived from many girls, from many churches, from many sonatas, will combine to form a single sonata, a single church, a single girl." There we read the origin of the Vinteuil sonata, of Saint-Hilaire, and of Albertine.

These thoughts lead Marcel inevitably to the conclusion of the novel, related to *le drame de mon coucher* when he had heard the sounds of M. Swann's departure. "I had heard the garden gate open, give a peal of its bell and close." *J'avais entendu la porte du jardin s'ouvrir, sonner, se refermer.*

Like a motif on these last pages, the word *mon livre* returns over and over again: the book whose subject matter came to him from Swann. He analyses this thought meticulously. That is why I call it a sermon text, lending itself to study and interpretation. Swann is seen here to be the dominant figure in Marcel's life. Swann's daughter Gilberte was his first love. Swann aroused in him the desire to go to Balbec. If he had not gone to Balbec, he might never have met Albertine and several Guermantes. He might never have met Elstir. It is a passage of gratitude to Swann for his knowledge of Balbec. He insists that he finally got to know the Guermantes Way because he had first known Swann's way.

Thanks to the sympathy, the advice, the example of Swann, Marcel, at the end of *Le Temps retrouvé,* and Marcel Proust in 1908, began the momentous journey into the past that absorbed all of his energy and all of his genius. He wrote a work of art that was undoubtedly at the same time an act of expiation. This duality may not be exceptional. I tend to believe that many masterpieces in all the arts may have their genesis in a will to expiate. I sense this in the Ninth Symphony, in Fra Angelico's *Annunciation* in Florence, in the cathedral of Chartres, yes, even in *Ulysses* of Joyce. Beauty does more than embellish life. It is a Reality (as Proust might say) more important than life.

This thought, so pervasive throughout the work, is often joined with a seemingly contradictory moral theory: the world seen as a baffling maze of illusions. It is apparent in what is for me the most tragic passage of the novel when Swann, condemned to death by a specialist, visits his great friend the duchess, and is forced to tell her of his illness. Oriane refuses to believe him and thus spoil her evening of three social events. More than merely an example of the Guermantes' egoism and self-centeredness, it is cruelty, unconscious cruelty which does infest the universe of *A la Recherche*. It does not poison it wholly. Life survives, after all. The Proustian characters have an unusual resilience, and yet almost all of them are at bay, in some form.

In such passages Proust seems to be saying that man is compact of ambiguities. These are the contradictions and contrasts in human nature, the heights and depths of human nature. "Cruelty" would seem to be the Proustian synonym for "pride," the gravest of all sins.

In the mid-point of the novel, in *Sodome et Gomorrhe,* the evening reception given by the Prince and Princesse de Guermantes, Proust draws his final portrait of Swann, whom I would call, without much hesitation, his favorite character. The background of the portrait is Swann's suffering from a mortal illness and from the Dreyfus Affair. His strength now is his solidarity with his race.

Proust rarely exhibits any preference, but I believe he does here in this last appearance of Swann, when he is saying to us that a race does not alter its attributes. In that long episode of the reception we have an outstanding example of Proust's skill in chronicling a social milieu at a given moment in history. It is also filled with passages of self-examination. In its center, with the figure of Swann, as he speaks to the Prince or to Marcel, we move far back into the past of an ancient ancestry, and ahead into the future where we faintly foresee a renewed suffering of that race. Swann appears in the passage as an ancient Hebrew prophet. And Proust, as the author of the passage, appears as the prophet of the increasingly complex world of modern man. In his novel, Proust moves away from materialism and positivism as explanations of the world, and attempts to explain the world in terms of society, history, art . . . and God.

I often think of this scene as one of crossroads, important *carrefours,* where the novelist insists on the subconscious recesses of a man's inner life, and at the same time rehearses themes of history and literature.

Like most teachers of Proust, I remind my students, when we are reading the entire work, that the opening pages on *Combray* are never really absent from the rest of the novel. Combray, in which Swann plays a reserved quiet role, but indispensable for all that follows, returns to us like invigorating air of the countryside. There we see peasants, a country doctor, a lady hastening to mass and hoping to get there before the Elevation, shopkeepers, a grocery boy adding to his principal job many others.

This return, this reiteration of Combray, may help explain a mysterious statement made at the end of Iris Murdoch's recent novel, her twenty-second novel, *The Good Apprentice,* of 1985. I have always felt that her art of fiction is close to Proust's. In the passage on the last page of her book, she refers specifically to Proust. It is a reunion scene between a father and his two grown sons. Harry, the father, asks his son Edward,

> "What's that book you're reading?" "Oh—Proust." Edward had been looking for the passage about Albertine going out in the rain on her bicycle, but he couldn't find it. He had turned to the beginning. *Longtemps je me suis couché de bonne heure.* What a lot of pain there was in those first pages. What a lot of pain there was all the way through. So how was it that the whole thing could vibrate with such a pure joy? This was something which Edward was determined to find out.

I have never encountered in any other book such a statement about the "pure joy" vibrating throughout Proust's book. But I do recognize that undercurrent of joy that rises from the sheer creating of the work. In an interview-article on this recent novel, published in *L'Express,* as Murdoch discusses other novelists: Henry James, Dostoievsky, Tolstoi,— she indicates that Proust is her favorite novelist, *Il est mon préféré.*

If I ever attempted to explain that "joy vibrating throughout the novel," I would turn to Swann. Not so much to his character, as to his spirit, which is something truer than character. His spirit is both mysterious and constructive. He is powerful with natural wealth. I mean the wealth of nature. The words used by Proust to describe Swann and his actions and his charm, flow through those pages like a river that brings sweet water to us, the readers. His scenes with Marcel, with Odette, with the Prince, with Oriane, with Gilberte, are scenes of crosspollenizing, as if he were the sun in the sky, drawing out what is hidden, and causing it to flower as if it were a heliotrope.

In this novel of one million words, the artist is the man who regains time. The famous flashback of *Un Amour de Swann* is the first elaborate example. After his marriage with Odette, Swann becomes a passionless husband, proud of her beauty, proud that Odette attracts so many men to "her day."

But Swann is not a true artist—no extra-temporal recognition comes to him. Long after his death, at the final matinée, Odette looks much as she ever did. Life had given her some good parts. The Swann-Odette story prefigures the Marcel-Albertine story in somewhat the same way that the Old Testament prefigures the New Testament, for medieval and Renaissance exegetes.

It would seem that in Proust's mind, Marcel and Swann are linked, joined in sensibility, in ambition, and in the place they occupy in the Faubourg Saint-Germain, despite their birth and their early lack of social connections. The temperamental affinities between Swann and Marcel are sketched at the beginning of the novel and are clearly heard at the end of the novel in the sound of the bell. Proust needed both Marcel and Swann in order to reveal the paradoxical character of our human condition, and thus to humanize the universe. To humanize it and also to discover in it its mystical origins.

A few of the recent critics (I am thinking of Jefferson Humphries), as well as some of the older critics (Fernandez, for example, and Cattaui), find in Proust traces of orphism and the religion of the gnostics—that is, traces of Greek antiquity and the first two centuries of Christianity. It is expressed in a nostalgia for a return to a primitive unity, or in a mourning over the fear that this primitive unity has been lost. Gérard de Nerval, one of Proust's favorite authors, had felt this in his effort to pierce "those gates of ivory and horn that separate us from the invisible world" (*ces portes d'ivoire et de corne qui nous séparent du monde invisible.*)

The word "metamorphosis" could serve as title for the novel in designating the cycle of *Temps perdu* and *Temps retrouvé*. The final appearance of Swann is almost a transfiguration. An impressionist painter like Elstir, so sympathetic to Swann, could not look at a flower without transplanting it in the interior garden of his mind. As Swann listened to *la petite phrase* of Vinteuil's sonata, and, much later, as Marcel listened to Vinteuil's septet, each drew an experience, a new understanding of experience, from the silence and the dark that surrounded the compositions. Vinteuil's music reawakened both Swann (in *Un Amour de Swann*) and Marcel (in *La Prisonnière*).

Several generations of educated American youth (educated if they take the right courses) have grown up in what I would call a Proustian climate. For the final exam in my Proust course, I list for one question three or four major characters and ask the students to write a portrait of one of those characters and discuss his or her important scenes. If Swann is on the list, and he usually is, 80-85 percent of the students choose him. They like Swann. They feel secure with him. He is one of the few characters who do not shift their sexual preference.

In this haunting gallery of characters that Proust gives us, tragic and ludicrous characters, I find that Charlus is the incomparable character in this work of fiction. And yet, Swann shows Proust's power of character presentation and delineation. Swann in a blend of several persons observed in reality. Marcel as a child senses the mystery that surrounds Swann. He is excited by this mysteriousness, and throughout the story he accumulates contradictions in this friend and counselor. Behind Swann is Proust who unites in himself contradictory qualities. Proust's penetration into a man's emotions and thoughts—I am thinking especially of Swann—is hardly equaled anywhere.

I often ask myself—and also my students on days when they seem eager to contradict me—what gave Proust this power of penetration. . . I would call it the power of imagination—that goddess imagination worshipped by Coleridge, Poe, Baudelaire, and Proust. Imagination—I am thinking again of *Un Amour de Swann*—constitutes the whole of love, according to Proust. If I take this thought one step farther, I would claim that imagination, enriched by a transfiguring memory, transmutes vices and jealousies into Beauty, into joy, if I use Iris Murdoch's word.

Every time I read Swann's love affair with Odette, I am struck by the details of that narrative. As a reader continues with the other parts of the novel, Swann's love for Odette turns almost into a myth that loses its realism with the passage of time. And yet it is there, expanded into the other love affairs. They are bigger stories, as Swann's love turns into a miniature. In terms of their love, Swann and Odette are mythicized. Swann, like Don Giovanni in Leporello's notebook, is remembered for his number of love affairs with seamstresses and *midinettes*. Odette is remembered as *la grande cocotte* that she was, with her many pasts each one of which provided her with a different name.

We read that Odette was not Swann's type. So he transformed her into Zipporah, a wife of Moses, as painted by Botticelli. This was carried out by the power of imagination. Swann talks not so much about the character or actions of Odette, as about her love of flowers, of orchids and chrysanthemums. Marcel, in his love for Odette, continues to relate her to flowers. He saw her first across the hawthorn hedge lining Tansonville. And later, going farther than Swann in this comparison of Odette with flowers, Marcel sees in its flowers and flowering trees, the Bois de Boulogne as the Elysian Garden of Woman, because Madame Swann has walked there.

The hawthorns and the lilacs of Swann's Way form one part of what I think we can call the Dantesque voyage of the narrator through his childhood and his loves, his *Vita Nuova*. The emblematic flowers are as important, in the formative years of Marcel, as the spires of Martinville and the medieval stone faces of Saint-André-des-Champs.

Recently in a museum on examining several paintings of Marc Chagall, I was struck by the theme of childhood they draw upon. Bridal couples, fiddlers, scrolls of the Torah, were the milieu of childhood from which the painter had never escaped. And I thought then of childhood so important in *Swann's Way*.

Childhood for Marcel was undisturbed by wars and revolutions. It was a time of great events, of great figures, especially great actresses, close at hand in a world still radiant and mysterious, yet so real that when he read Genesis, the boy could embrace the angels of Abraham. This thought of childhood in the paintings of Chagall and in the text of Proust, reminded me that they bear witness to greater knowledge than Proust and Chagall possessed, unconscious knowledge, patriarchal knowledge.

Archetypal symbols of Chagall: the moon, the bride, the angel; and the archetypal symbols of Proust: the madeleine cakes of Léonie, the cattleyas of Odette, the stone faces of Saint-André, caused me to reflect that the feminine dominates Chagall's paintings and *A la recherche*. The understanding strength of the grandmother, and the life story of Mme de Villeparisis control and delight the attentiveness of Marcel as much as any male figure in the story, even Swann.

In the chapter of *Combray,* when Marcel tries to tell us how important the two ways are for him, he describes them as a fragment of landscape (*morceau de paysage*) that floats uncertainly in his mind like a flowering Delos (the Greek island which once floated before Zeus attached it). A few pages before this passage, Marcel watches a water lily, helpless in the current of the Vivonne, and he thinks not only of Léonie, unable to move from her bed, but also of the spirits in Dante's hell, unable to leave their circle. The passage ends with reference to Virgil, Dante's guide who has to urge him on to the next circle.

My students study first the role of Virgil as guide to Dante, and then when they read Proust, it is not hard for them to consider Swann as Marcel's guide comparable to Virgil in the *Commedia*. Swann leads Marcel to woman: to Odette, first, and then to Gilberte, and then indirectly to Albertine.

Like many readers of Proust, I have come to look upon the goodnight kiss episode as the cornerstone of the entire novel. As a dinner guest that night, Swann at first deprives Marcel of his mother's kiss. But then a reversal takes place, and because of Swann, Marcel is more indulged in than ever, when his mother spends that night in his room. We might conclude therefore that Swann leads to the mother, representing all women, as Virgil leads Dante to Beatrice in the *Divine Comedy*.

Contributors

Anne Borrel, who received her doctorate from the Sorbonne, created the Institut Marcel Proust international (IMPi) in 1988, as a section of the Société des Amis de Marcel Proust et des Amis de Combray (SAMP). She was granted a leave from her teaching post by the French Minister of Education to serve as the secretary-general of SAMP and IMPi. The purpose of IMPi is to create a data base of Proustian publications and activities around the world and to develop and promote them.

Roger Shattuck holds a faculty appointment in the University Professors Program at Boston University. Author of six books, plus a number of translations and editions of well-known French writers, he often contributes poems to magazines such as *The Saturday Review*, *Harper's*, and *The Hudson Review*; he frequently contributes essays and reviews to *The New York Review of Books*. He has written two books on Marcel Proust, *Proust's Binoculars* and *Marcel Proust*, which won the 1975 National Book Award for critical biography.

Elyane Dezon-Jones teaches French literature at Barnard College. She is the author of *Proust et l'Amérique* (Paris: Nizet, 1982), *Marcel Proust: La Figure des pays* in collaboration with photographer François Xavier Bouchart (Colona, 1982) and the editor-in-chief of the *Bulletin Marcel Proust*. She edited *The Guermantes Way* for the new Flammarion edition of *Remembrance of Things Past* and is currently working on a theory of genetic criticism. She also published an anthology of French women writers, *Les Ecritures féminines* (Magnard, 1983), and a book on Marie de Gournay, *Fragments d'un discours féminin* (Corti, 1988).

Nathalie Mauriac Dyer is one of the editors of the second part of *Sodome et Gomorrhe III,* on which Proust was working in the year of his death and for which he used the title "Albertine disparue" (*Albertine disparue,* ed. N. Mauriac et E. Wolff, Paris, Editions B. Grasset, 1987). This revised version of the text that Robert Proust, Mrs. Dyer's great-grandfather, and Jacques Rivière inaccurately published under that title in 1925 came to light only in 1986, as is described by Claude Mauriac in *L'oncle Marcel* (Grasset, 1988). Nathalie Dyer is currently engaged in a dissertation in the field of Greek literature and in further work on Proust's final intentions for *Sodome et Gomorrhe III, IV.*

Richard M. Ratzan is an Associate Professor of Medicine at the University of Connecticut School of Medicine where he has taught medical humanities for the past ten years. His particular field of interest is the intersection of literature and ethics. Dr. Ratzan is the past president of the William Carlos Williams Society.

J. Theodore Johnson, Jr., grandson of a woodcarver and son of a painter, works in the area of the interrelations of the arts in France with specific focus on literature and painting. He is founding editor of the *Proust Research Association Newsletter* published at the University of Kansas where he has been Professor of French since 1968. He participated as Jemison Visiting Professor in the Marcel Proust program at the University of Alabama at Birmingham, fall term, 1988.

Jean Milly, after having held faculty appointments at the Universities of Nancy and Amiens, began his research on Proust's pastiches and style in 1972. He is currently Professor of French at the Sorbonne Nouvelle, where he is director of the Center for Proustian Studies. Having been sent as an exchange professor to many foreign countries, he was most recently Visiting Professor at the City

University of New York. Professor Milly is the General Editor of the new ten-volume Garnier-Flammarion edition of *A la recherche du temps perdu*. He is the editor of two of the volumes in that collection, *La Prisonnière* and *La Fugitive*.

Philip Kolb, Professor Emeritus, University of Illinois at Urbana-Champaign, established the basis of Proustian chronology in his doctoral dissertation, providing a chronology and a critical commentary of Proust's published correspondence (Harvard, 1938). This was published in 1949 and awarded a medal and a diploma in 1951 by the French Academy. At that time, Proust's niece asked him to undertake a new general edition of the correspondence. The first volume, published in 1970, was awarded a Grand Prix by the French Academy. Volume 17 was recently published, and volumes 18 and 19 will appear soon. Professor Kolb was appointed a member of the Order of the French Legion of Honor, with rank of Chevalier, in 1983.

Wallace Fowlie, born in Brookline, Massachusetts, in 1908, educated at Harvard (A.B., A.M., Ph.D.), has taught French literature and Dante at Harvard, Yale, the University of Chicago, and Bennington College. Since 1964 he has been James B. Duke professor of Romance Studies at Duke University. In addition to his critical books on Proust, Mallarmé, Rimbaud, and Dante, he has translated works of Molière, Rimbaud, and Saint-John Perse. His fourth volume of memoirs will be published in 1989 (Duke University Press), as well as a brief history of French Symbolism (Penn State University Press).